The author proudly supports the Christopher and Dana Reeve Foundation, dedicated to curing spinal cord injury by funding innovative research and improving the quality of life for people living with paralysis through grants, information, and advocacy.

The Christopher and Dana Reeve Foundation is a registered 501©(3) nonprofit organization designated by the Internal Revenue Code. All contributions made to it are fully tax-deductible. Gifts may be sent to Reeve Foundation, 636 Morris Turnpike, Suite 3A, Short Hills, NJ 07078.

More info at <u>christopherreeve.org</u>.

Don't Fight with the Garden Hose

and Other Lessons I've Learned Along the Way

Tom Harvey

Copyright © 2013 by Tom Harvey

All Rights Reserved. No part of this book may be reproduced or transmitted in any form or by any means, electronic or mechanical, including photocopying, recording, or by any information storage and retrieval system, without written permission from the publisher, except by a reviewer who may quote brief passages in a review.

Just Load The Wagon Publishing
PO Box 2093
Kirkland, WA 98083

When You Believe lyrics written by Stephen Lawrence Schwartz. Published by DWA Songs. All rights reserved. Used with permission.

Arther Fox genealogy courtesy of Steven Williams at usgwarchives.org. Used with permission.

Cover design by Ian Pamplona at Ian.Pamplona@gmail.com.

LIBRARY OF CONGRESS
CATALOGING-IN-PUBLICATION DATA
has been applied for.
Library of Congress Control Number:
2012913546

ISBN 10: 0982874235

ISBN 13: 978-0-9828742-3-3

ISBN e-version: 978-0-9828742-4-0

PRINTED IN THE UNITED STATES OF AMERICA

"The Eighties:
A Bitchen Time To Be a Teenager!"
is available exclusively
for the Kindle app
at www.Amazon.com

Double Secret Probation

thanks to
the Harvey Family's
personal
Superman:

Lance Beauchamp

The author, Superman Lance, and David Harvey.
Lance read "Do Not Stand at My Grave and Weep"
at our mother's funeral and I love the guy for it.
(December 5, 2008)

Thanks to the guys
who make me laugh
every single day:

David
Lorne
Jim Holmes
Ramiro Rodriguez
Dios Chaz Serame
Sherman Smith
Michael Wells

Memorable quotes

Well, what a day for a daydream!

— Bono talking to the Paris crowd after the live version of *Party Girl*

● ● ●

You are driving me hilarious!

and

I didn't know it was a crime to be hungry!
(when she wanted a bowl of cereal at 10:00 p.m.)

— Chloe, the 13-going-on-30-year-old in the family

Note

I have a fondness for footnotes but don't like how detached they are in e-format. Therefore, I've converted the footnotes to text that appear in brackets. For e-readers, this will save you going back and forth between the text and the footnotes section at the back of the book.

Table of Contents

	Prologue	xvii
1:	Don't fight with the garden hose, it doesn't care if it loses!	1
2:	You are absolutely forbidden!	7
3.	*Le Ballon Rouge*	11
4:	February 9-12, 1978, or *The news*	17
5:	Don't mess with a mother's love, or *Don't be a dick to your little sister*	25
6:	Brushes with the spirit world, aka WTF was *that*?	31
	• The Haunted Glass	33
	• The Haunted Pitcher	34
	• The Haunted Lamp	35
7:	*Eighties* outtakes	39
8:	Ode to Odie: Don't sweat the small stuff, just load the wagon!	49
8a:	Odie in the Kill Zone	61
9:	Stars walk among us	65
10:	That the Paul David Hewson urinal?	71
11:	The visit	77
12:	Damon Wayans is right	85
13:	JC, my favorite DJ	89

14:	Choosing a doctor for your annual male exam. Yes, that *exam!*	97
15:	You will stand on your mother's grave	103
16:	Goodbye Gunkles	109
17:	If it were easy everyone would do it	135
18:	Musings	147
	• Leggo My Eggo!	147
	• Uh, it's a *hand* dryer . . .	148
	• The *famous* Sonny Sanders	149
	• To all you public nose blowers . . .	151
	• That thing has *how many* calories?	153
	• *Other* Tom Harveys	156
	• Leave it to the automotive industry!	157
	• Just because you *can* doesn't mean you *should*	158
	• Conquering *The Omega Man*	161
	• Keep turning the corner, Bryan(s)	164
19:	Tom the terrorist	169
20:	What every 14-year-old should know	179
21:	What's *your* personal mix tape?	185
22:	Parting words from Arther Fox	193
23:	*The Little Boy*	197
24:	Parting thoughts	199
	• Books Read Along The Way	201
	• Acknowledgements	203
	• Homage To a Friend	205

Prologue

I learned quite a bit about writing, rewriting, editing, (and editing, and editing some more) via my 2012 memoir chronicling growing up in the 1980s. *Really* eye-opening stuff like, You can't just shove a book at someone and say, *Here read this!*

Time is valuable. Time is *precious.*

I sent fifty copies of *The Eighties* to my friends. All of them thanked me. Not all of them actually read it but at least they were polite about it.

The Kindle version went viral with nearly 15,000 downloads when I offered it for free in May, 2012, and people from *all over the world* continue to email me with encouraging messages. Davi Tavares from Rio, God bless you brother!

This was truly amazing since I had my doubts whether anyone would be interested in reading about a stranger growing up in *No Man's Land, California* (as in *Central California* . . . is it Northern California? Southern California? To be honest, I still don't know myself).

But more than anything I was humbled. Humbled that people of all ages and walks of life would take their *precious time* to read about the life, loves, and losses of a total stranger.

The greatest writer of fiction, Mr. Stephen King himself, calls us *Constant Reader*.

I like that.

If you're a Constant Reader of mine then you humble me to the core.

Thank you for that.

Seriously, thank you.

• • •

To follow is a collection of stories, thoughts, and reflections I've picked up along my 45-year journey, mostly in chronological order. If you don't find a shred of it useful, I hope I've at least forced a laugh on you.

Maybe when you least expect it.

Or maybe you'll shed a tear.

God knows I do both every single time I read my own writing.

Every single time.

1

Don't fight with the garden hose, it doesn't care if it loses!

Nowadays they come in all different colors—black, orange, red, grey, light green, dark green, *neon turquoise*—in any number of lengths and circumferences.

Hell, you can buy them full of holes if you want.

And stacked neatly in the aisles of Home Depot and Lowes, they look so *benign*.

So clean.

So helpful.

To be honest, they look damn near sexy for the images they provoke: lush, green lawns and spotless cars in driveways.

This tool, this thing of beauty, this *garden hose* holds so much promise.

Were I capable of traveling back in time and befriending George Orwell, the last four words of *1984* would read, *He loved garden hoses*. That's how much I've come to respect them.

Growing up in the stifling heat of Central California has a lot to do with it. Turn the nozzle and cool, clear water splashed our parched faces. Hook it to a sprinkler and we had an instant front-yard party. Squirt big brother then run like hell in search of Mom's legs to hide behind. X-Box, Playstation, Wii–we knew of no such things.

But make no bones about it, Satan himself was chief architect in Hell's plumbing department. While the hose *looks* helpful–*innocently* coiled waiting for you on the shelf or in the yard–there is an inherent *evil* about it.

The thing's *gonna* kink.

Whether you're washing the car or watering the bushes, it's *gonna* kink. And not just in one place, it's gonna kink *every four feet*.

At this point you have two options.

Option One:

The Wild West Lasso Whip. Using the car-washing example, this option *will* result in:

a) Smacking the very car you're trying to clean.
b) Knocking your three-year-old niece to her knees, an innocent bystander listening for *The*

Entertainer blasting from the ice cream truck one street over.
c) Cracking yourself in the face resulting in a bloody nose.
d) All of the above.

Regardless of the result, the kink in the hose *will* remain (a scientifically-proven fact). *Evil*, man. I'm telling you, *evil!*

Rather than subject yourself to any or all of these outcomes, allow me to offer the following advice:

When it comes to hose-handling become a *pacifist.*
Become *friends* with the hose.
Empathize with the hose.

Option Two:

When the hose kinks (and it *will* kink, we've already established that), take a deep breath and thank God for the simple things in life. Thank Him for, say, the fact that the ice cream truck driver got a job unloading UPS trucks and gave up his ice cream route.

Find your inner peace and calmly unkink the hose, for Human Logic dictates that the hose *is an inanimate object!* It *doesn't* have a brain. It's not *trying* to piss you off! Be the bigger of the two and you'll be better off.

Nowadays, it pays to apply Garden Hose Logic in a broader context for circumstances beyond our control.

Examples include:

- Don't let grief consume your life for too long when you lose her. Remember the good times–and there were many–because that's what your mom would want.
- Don't expect to sleep through the night while camping at a Washington State park. When the piercing scream of the crying baby shatters camp at 2 a.m. it's a great time to fire up *Dark Side of the Moon* on your iPod. (And do give credit to the guy who screams, "Shut that damn baby up!" And the response, "Come over here and make me MFer!")
- Don't blame the dog for the sudden change in breathable oxygen after sharing a bag of pork rinds with him. On second thought, go ahead and blame the dog.
- Don't expect to get a good night's sleep when you let your twenty-pound dog on the king-size bed. Canine physics dictate that, in the dark, the dog *will* morph into a Great Dane and you *will* wake up feeling like you've slept in a baby crib. Double the sense of dread if you've just finished a bag of pork rinds with him.
- Don't blame *the cop* for your speeding ticket going through Pleasant Valley, Oregon (especially if you're in a Ryder Truck driving, one-way, across the country). *Thank* him for keeping the completely deserted stretch of road safe from lawbreakers.

- Don't be angry with the driver in the Nissan Leaf who cuts into the onramp-merge-lane at the very last second (after you've been crawling along for nearly a mile). Actually, go ahead and be pissed. *Be very pissed!*

> Garden Hose Lesson Learned:
> Beware the kinky hose!

2

You are absolutely forbidden!

Within ten minutes of Lorne bringing it home, Cheech and Chong's *Los Cochinos* album had been thoroughly inspected and summarily confiscated.

"You are absolutely forbidden from listening to this," stepdad, Metro, said with his usual air of superiority. The front of the album, depicting the hippie-like duo of Cheech Marin and Tommy Chong, wasn't *that* incriminating. Opening the album, however, spelled our doom: depictions of marijuana stashed in various door panels.

The year was 1976 and Lorne, all of twelve years old, wasn't doing us any favors by bringing home humor of the *illicit drug variety*.

The three Harvey brothers slumped in our chairs with the same expression the kid wore when he was told he'd shoot his eye out in *A Christmas Story*. We were *bummed* and thinking the same thing, *Dumb Meatball! We never have any fun!*

Satisfied with the disappointment on our faces, Meathead climbed the stairs and stashed the album in the master bedroom as we huddled in the living room.

"We'll get that album back," Lorne whispered.

David nodded.

"Yeah, next time he's at sea we'll find it for sure."

For twelve and ten, my brothers were pretty cool.

The eight year old in the group (that would be me) looked at them in awe. Oh, the *defiance!*

Meatstick was in the Coast Guard and away from home for weeks at a time. As long as he didn't break the record in pieces, our Search and Rescue plan had a high probability of success.

And so it took about a day for the proclamation, *You are absolutely forbidden from listening to this,* to morph into, *You will listen to this non-stop in my absence.*

That's really the point of this chapter.

If you forbid something from someone, you're likely to hurl them at it with the grit, determination and fearlessness of a bullfighter in the *Plaza de Toros La Malagueta* (the wickedly-cool bull fighting ring in Spain).

So the next time Meatsack's dumb ship went on maneuvers, the Harvey brothers went in search of our forbidden fruit, the album known as *Los Cochinos*.

It took all of five minutes with three sets of eyes scouring the master bedroom.

"Got it!" David exclaimed, reversing himself from the closet on his hands and knees, the album wedged in his teeth. "It was propped up in the back of the closet. What a dumb hiding place!"

Passing Mom on the stairs (we were streaming down, she was coming up), we huddled around the record player in the living room and put the needle to the record.

Mom called down, "Be sure you put that back in the *exact* place you found it!"

What a cool mom.

"We will!" I shouted happily.

"Duh," David whispered.

• • •

Nowadays you could put a gun to my head and demand that I sing *The Star Spangled Banner* and, with my life on the line, I'd be doomed. *Whose broad stripes and bright stars thru the perilous night (?) . . . fight (?) . . . gave proof (?) . . . truth (?) through the night . . .* I honestly don't know for sure.

The fact that I don't know the words to the National Anthem is kicked up a notch on the Absurdity Scale once I admit that I can recite *Los Cochinos* word for word.

All forty three minutes of useless 1970s weed humor. *Word for word.*

Even though I haven't listened to it in over thirty years.

So to all you parents out there, remember this:

The next time you *absolutely forbid* something from your kid, know that you are arming him or her with energy drawn from the far corners of the cosmos. I'm not saying you should not be the best parent you can be– and this discussion has *nothing* to do with marijuana advocacy–all I'm saying is that you're going to have to outsmart your smart kid.

Maybe a little reverse psychology, but what do I know? I have a degree in history.

> Garden Hose Lesson Learned:
> Kids are a lot smarter than we give them credit for. Enough said.

3

Le Ballon Rouge

Perusing the Bellevue Goodwill, I found the book. Or, perhaps, it found me.

In either case, it was the discovery of a lifetime–this treasure–priced at 99 cents: *The Red Ballon* by Albert Lamorisse. If you're not familiar with it, the simple story involves a possessed balloon that won't leave a little boy's side in 1950s Paris.

To my surprise, the book was published in 1956. The scribble on the inside cover added to my sense of awe:

"For Confirmation, Christine Schneider, May 25, 1962."

Based on this, I'm guessing that Christine, if she's alive, is now eligible for Medicare. I wonder, did she tire of the book? Did she die? How did this treasure find its way to me among the dusty, musty smell of the Bellevue Goodwill? How long did it sit on the shelf before I happened upon it? Does anyone else care about *The Red Ballon*?!

I saw the film in the 2nd grade at Red Hill Elementary School in Honolulu, Hawaii. Back in 1976, movies in the classroom were noisy films on clunky reels that usually started with the same one-minute anti-pollution ad.

The Indian in his orange calfskin outfit canoeing through the sludge. He beaches the boat and ends up standing next to a freeway (*WTH?*) where someone violently splatters a Happy Meal on his clean moccasins. The short film fades out with a tear streaking down Iron Eyes Cody's chiseled face. Clearly, the guy is *not* amused.

Good grief people, if you didn't like the Happy Meal why the hell did you order it?

I never understood why old Iron Eyes was the face of an anti-pollution campaign. It was about this time we were learning about the plight of the American Indian; namely, that they got hosed at every opportunity by white settlers and the US Calvary. If our forefathers didn't give a rat's butt about Chief Watery Eye, why would a bunch of school kids?

Picture *this* for an anti-pollution film:

Arthur Fonzarelli flying over the bars of his motorcycle after crashing into a discarded box spring in the road. In the next scene, he has a butterfly bandage over his eyebrow, a black eye, and a cast on his left arm. As the voice over says *Littering is not cool!* the Fonz gives us a vehement thumbs down. As the film fades to black, a Happy Meal splatters his brown leather jacket. Now that *would have* been cool in 1976.

Among the warpy orchestral sounds of violins, clarinets and kettle drums, *Le Ballon Rogue,* whisked the wide-eyed Red Hill 2nd graders to another time–another place–at least for the next half hour. The film entranced us and we happily watched it multiple times that school year. War-torn Paris was *so damn dreary* and the balloon was the brightest, most candy-apple-red thing we'd ever seen. We couldn't get enough of that big, beautiful latex monstrosity. Never mind that it was *never* the same balloon from scene to scene–its size and string length constantly changed–we got the point.

After reading the book with as much reverence possible in the noisy office, I took the plunge and watched the film–37 years removed from the darkened Red Hill classroom–on YouTube. For a movie with almost no dialogue other than "Bah-loon! Bah-loon!"–the book explained some of the strangeness. Things like:

Who's the grumpy old guy in the black suit?

Answer (from the book): The principal of the elementary school.

Why did he lock the kid up?

Answer (from the book): The kid got locked in the principal's office because the *bah-loon* disrupted class and our little protagonist did nothing to help the situation. Now, seriously, don't you think the Fire Marshall or Child Protective Services would take issue with locking a kid up for most of the school day? What mischief could he have caused?

While watching the movie on my laptop in my cubicle over lunch, I found it hard to sit still. Much like the film-projector scene in *The Shawshank Redemption* where the convicts hurl catcalls at the Rita Hayworth movie, *Gilda*, I found myself suppressing my own outbursts of dialogue at this mostly-dialogue-less French film.

The kid can't get on the streetcar (No balloons allowed! Hey, I didn't see the sign!) and is left standing in the middle of the busy street. The camera moves in on a close-up of the kid's blank face.

Don't you leave me in the street! I'm just a little kid for Chrissake! Hey, I'm talking to you!

Second day of school.

Mom, I am the only kid wearing sweats to school. Jesus, can't you buy me a pair of corduroys?

Boy with red balloon crosses paths with girl with blue balloon.

Hey baby, where you headed on this dreary day?

The band of roving, balloon-killing white boys give chase.

Get away from me you buncha losers!

Mom and kid go to church.

Mom, I'm still wearing these crappy, gray sweats. Do you seriously think the blazer, shirt, and tie go with them? Maman, j'ai l'air d'un assclown total!

[Translation: Mom, I look like a total assclown!]

The kid blows off his mom after getting thrown out of church.

That's one way to get out of church! I'm going to buy a pastry with the money I was supposed to put in the collection plate! (Another question answered from the book, thanks!)

The band of roving, balloon-killing white boys give chase, AGAIN, and little Jean-Phillipe (hell, that name works, right?) takes flight.

Don't make me do a Rambo and flat blast all of y'all! I will pull out my Swiss Army Knife and carve you all new . . . well, you get the idea.

Oh, the poor red balloon finally meets its doom from the aforementioned mob of slingshot-slinging Parisian boys (who are all, now, in their late sixties and likely doing time for aggravated assault in some leaky French jail). But our hero balloon doesn't just pop–it takes nearly a minute to *slowly* die a tortuous death before some di*khead stomps on it. Seriously, how *rude!*

From here, every Parisian balloon abandons their kid to come to the aid of our poor little sweats-wearing-even-to-church Jean-Phillipe. To hell with the feelings of many–we're only worried about *our* boy. The credits roll and the film fades to black as he flies high above Paris. *Wee!*

But, wait.

The screen fades back in and as he rises higher and higher into the sky, the atmospheric pressure pops each balloon one by one until we see little Jean-Phillipe hurl face first back to the cobblestone street–arms and legs flailing–SPLAT! And in the ultimate insult, the little girl who lost her blue balloon snags the sweats off our little tragic hero's broken body–leaving him a bloody mass of pulp–showing his severely holey underwear.

THE END.

All right, so I have an overactive imagination.

Don't get me wrong, I still love the movie. I just want more for the little guy, that's all.

• • •

I had to laugh when I posted a collage of pictures from the movie on my Facebook community page (www.facebook.com/86kicks). In true form, someone posted: *Now all you need is 98 more balloons and we'd have a song about starting a nuclear war!*

Nice.

• • •

Note to Christine Schneider: I have your book if you'd like it back (and I hope your Confirmation went well).

> Garden Hose Lesson Learned:
> The imagination of an adult sometimes trumps that of a child.

4

February 9-12, 1978 or, *The news*

"February 8, 1978 was a Wednesday–my tenth birthday. The phone rang at 9:30 p.m., but David and I were already in our bunk bed for the night. We were awake–talking about the birthday party invitations we'd pass out the next day. Since our birthdays are three days apart, the party was scheduled for Saturday the 11th, David's twelfth birthday. In hushed tones, we heard our grandparents on the phone. When they told us the news the next day, we didn't pass out the invitations. The party was cancelled."

–previously published in *The Eighties*

For a day full of excitement (I was, after all, 10, and David was 11, meaning we were just *one year apart*, at least for the next two days), the grandparents were in a subdued mood. Like any other morning, we ate our cereal at the table while watching Good Morning America.

I carefully straightened my small stack of birthday party invitations. Invited guests included my favorite girl, Pam; my best friend, Leonard; Jim, Melanie; definitely not that bully, Joey.

Grandpa put his hand on my arm and quietly said, "Let's not have you pass out your invitations today."

"Why not?"

"Let's just have you hold onto them."

He looked over at Grandma sitting at the other end of the table.

"We have some news to share with you after school," she said.

"Good news or bad news?" I asked.

She smiled.

"Let's just wait until after school, OK?"

David and I walked the mile to Terra Bella Elementary wondering what the big brouhaha was all about. The morning was cold and quiet; the fog in full force.

At band practice that day, Mr. Vangsness threw up his hands and bellowed, "Stop! Stop! This sounds like a funeral march!" David made a note of this in a two page letter he wrote to himself the next day.

We were excited for the final school bell to ring–anxious to hear *the news* that awaited us. Was the divorce from Meatstick finally over? Was Mom finally leaving Hawaii with our sister?

We discussed the scenarios, in between gulps of breath, as we ran home. We patted John, the black Greyhound, and Killer, the red Doberman, on our way into the kitchen.

Our grandparents were in the exact spots we had left them eight hours earlier: Grandpa at his end of the table (the left side), Grandma on the other (the right side). *What was our schoolteacher grandmother doing home so early? Did she take the day off from Steve Garvey Junior High? This was highly unusual.*

"Well," I demanded, "tell us the news!"

"We have good news and we have bad news," Grandma said slowly. "Which do you want first?"

"The bad news," I said without hesitation. Bad news *first* meant good news *last!*

Our grandparents looked at each other. Grandpa's eyes flooded with tears. Grandma remained emotionless; expressionless.

"Let's start with the *good* news," Grandma replied. "First give me a big, strong hug."

I groaned and shuffled to her. She squeezed me hard and held on for what felt like an hour; her breath reeked of cigarettes and Polident. David got the better end of the deal with a bear hug from Grandpa–Grandpa had given up smoking years earlier.

My brother and I sat shoulder-to-shoulder on the same side of the table–David and Grandpa to my left, Grandma on my right.

"I want you boys to be strong," she said, "and the good news is that we expect your mother to come home any day now."

I groaned. *This wasn't news!* We had heard this dozens of times. *This was the good news?*

Grandpa wiped his eyes and blew his nose in his handkerchief. I looked at David out of the corner of my left eye. He was as confused as I was.

In her expressionless, monotone voice, Grandma continued.

"Your father's been in an accident..."

And there the words hung.

My immediate thought was, *He broke his leg.*

I pictured our blue-collar, tough guy dad with his leg in a full-length white cast.

He broke his leg. How did he do that? The image made me smile.

"...a *fatal* accident."

Although she only said those last three words once, the key word echoed in my mind: *fatal... fatal... fatal.*

Fatal... dead... final... his leg isn't broken... he's in a funeral home at this very moment.

My entire body went numb, a million tiny needles tingled the length of my body. I couldn't feel my hands. I couldn't feel my legs. The world began to spin and my numb hands grabbed the table for balance.

We sat in silence as the words and images took hold.

My next memory is later that evening. My brother leaned against the doorjamb, clutching the white receiver of the wall-mounted rotary phone. Mom was on the line and David cried uncontrollably. After a few minutes he handed me the phone.

"Make it fast," Grandma said. This was a speed call–long distance to Hawaii was expensive.

"How's my big, strong boy?" Mom asked weakly. Unable to form words, all I could do was wail into the phone.

Dad was dead. Mom was 2,500 miles away. All the ice cream in the world wasn't going to make this better.

Mom cried on the other end and said, "He loved you very much" and, "I'll be home just as soon as I can" and, "Be strong, baby."

We stayed home from school on Friday the 10th, meaning we had one school day off to deal with the news. There was no such thing as grief counseling or Camps For Kids With Dead Dads.

On Saturday I asked about the funeral. Grandma said it was Sunday.

"Aren't we going?"

"No. It's raining in Washington. Too dangerous to travel."

Raining in Washington? It's always raining in Washington! I was furious. The excuse was lame, even by a 10-year-old's standards, and they would have been better off with the truth: they weren't going to spend the money to fly us to Walla Walla and weren't interested in a 16-hour road trip.

We went to church on Sunday and Pastor Robin looked down on the Two Fatherless Boys from the pulpit with sadness in his eyes. After the service, he followed us home and Grandma made lunch. Our young, vibrant pastor with the bushy moustache told us that, "Your dad loved you guys very much."

How does he know that? He's never met the man. And he'll never meet the man.

David and I were happy for the company though– still pissed at our grandparents since the younger sons weren't allowed to go to their own father's funeral.

With the grieving period apparently over, we walked to school on Monday discussing various scenarios to explain the birthday party cancellation. We agreed that *Grandma had the flu* would be the most believable lie.

I walked into Mrs. Ward's 4th grade class and she patted me on the back–a hug would have created too many questions among my classmates.

"I'm so sorry," she whispered. "I'm sure your dad loved you very much."

That seems to be the general consensus.

"Are you still OK to preside over court today?"

Great.

Mock court.

I had volunteered to be the judge and missed Friday's instructions as to how the thing would proceed. The seating arrangement was such that Mrs. Ward's desk was now at the head of the classroom and that was to be my desk. Desks along the window were for the pre-selected jury. Two tables were setup for the Prosecution and Defense.

Everyone took their places and there I sat facing my 4th grade classmates. My best friend, Leonard, acting as the Bailiff, sat to my left. My favorite girl, Pam, sat in the front row, her face propped up in her palms. *She's proud of me*. We smiled at each other.

Mrs. Ward parked her big frame in one of the small desks in the back.

And there we sat.

Everyone looked at me. I looked back.

Yeah, I missed Friday because my dad accidently took a .357 hollow point to the chest at pointblank.
Missed out on the instructions.
I have no clue what's going on here.
Ten seconds passed. No one said a word.
Twenty seconds passed. No one said a word.
Finally, Mrs. Ward spoke up.
"Tom, perhaps if you ask the Prosecution to present the facts to the jury, we can proceed with this case."
Before I could stop myself, I cleared my throat and said,"Bailiff, if there's another outburst from the lady in the back of the room you will remove her from my court!"
Everyone turned to gauge Mrs. Ward's expression– one of pure shock. I was shocked that I said it but, hey, it was the grief talking.
I turned to Leonard.
"Bailiff . . . *Leonard!* Do you understand my instructions?"
Leonard, two shades whiter than he had been 5 seconds earlier, nodded. He looked *queasy*.
"Now, if the Prosecution would kindly present the facts to the jury, we can proceed with this case!"
I sat back and the day resumed like any other.

> Garden Hose Lesson Learned:
> Death doesn't care if it's your birthday
> or a holiday (say, *Thanksgiving?!*).
> Such is life.

5

Don't mess with a mother's love,
or
Don't be a dick to your little sister

At age 35, Mom found herself in the midst of her second divorce.

A perennial housewife since the age of 20, she had no marketable work skills other than self-taught jewelry creations (mainly puka shell necklaces which we sold at the Saturday-Drive-In-Turned-Swap Meet in Hawaii) and self-taught cake decorations (which she sold to the neighbors). She didn't have a college degree.

At a time when we would have received more on Public Assistance (aka Welfare) than what she earned at her part-time job at Montgomery Ward, she enrolled in the nursing program at Porterville Junior College. For two years, she went to class and the surrounding hospitals working toward her Licensed Practical Nursing license. And what a proud day it was when she graduated!

She used to say, *God doesn't give you too much that you can't handle.*

I suppose in the case of Patricia Ann Harvey, He threw a lot of life and strife at her, but she was resilient.

Between her paltry rate as an LPN (not much more than the minimum wage of $3.35 an hour at the time) and the Social Security we received as a result of Dad's sudden death, we managed. She did her absolute best, buying us bicycles when we really couldn't afford it; feeding the cookie jar with dollar bills which we'd promptly blow on video games after school; even scored my little sister a Cabbage Patch Kid when they were nearly unattainable.

One memory that always makes me chuckle *and* shed a tear involves my sister, Tricia.

The year was 1984. I was sixteen and my sister was nine.

Mom asked me to take Tricia shopping after my sister successfully lobbied for a new pair of shoes. The $25 Mom gave us was *twice* the budget of what I had spent on athletic cleats two years earlier.

[If you could call those crappy plastic ProWings *cleats*. I was the *only* kid on the freshman football team wearing them.]

And I'm not shy about saying that I was the most frugal kid in the family.

[Examples include not spending *any* of the money Mom gave us when we went to the movie theater. Or the year Mom bought David and I ridiculously overpriced

Oakley "Mumbo" sunglasses which I promptly had her return–well, my pair at least.]

Poor Tricia would have been better off with her *other* brother taking her shopping.

But back to the budget. $25 was nearly a full day's pay for our mother emptying bedpans, changing oozed-on, nasty dressings, and taking the abuse of stressed-out doctors. Twenty five dollars was *a lot* of money in 1984.

So Tricia and I strolled into Payless in search of shoes for a nine-year-old girl. After 15 minutes, it was apparent conflict was on the horizon.

The $9 pair I found looked just fine to me.

The $23 pair Tricia picked out (knee-high boots with obnoxious faux fur wrapped around the top) was the only pair that was acceptable. Naturally she found the most expensive pair of shoes in the store.

Keep in mind that we're talking Central California where, in the summer, the temperature hit 100 degrees by 9 a.m. Why the hell Payless Shoes sold furry knee-high boots in Porterville, California, *in the summer*, is still a mystery to me.

The nine-year-old was Hell Bent Determined that the boots were hers.

The frugal sixteen-year-old didn't share her opinion.

"We. Are. Poor. If you haven't noticed," I scolded her, thinking she'd fall in line and be satisfied with the crappy, cheap pair I picked out.

"I. Want. *These!*" she screamed and held up the boots.

"I'm making the decision here and I say you can spend ten bucks."

"Mom gave you twenty five!"

"Mom *did* give me twenty five and I intend on giving her most of it back! Now, do you want a new pair of shoes or not?"

My sister's face distorted into what can only be described as *pure rage with a massive dose of tortuous pain*–I saw this look once before after she came home to her Cabbage Patch doll hanging by a noose, a homemade death certificate pinned over the birth certificate. Her ensuing tantrum in the middle of Payless Shoes did nothing to sway my position. In fact, her fury only solidified my position that, *she was getting the $9 pair come hell or high water!*

We left the store with me carrying the shoes, since she refused to touch them, and her wailing in the car all the way home.

It was the longest five minutes in a car I've ever known.

When we got home, I gave Mom the change and Tricia stormed into the master bedroom wailing to high heaven. Mom disappeared after her to find out what all the fuss was about. I promptly went into my room and put the needle to Def Leppard's *Pyromania* album, determined to put the whole ordeal behind me.

Kids!
Little sisters!
Argh!

The next day Tricia pranced, danced, and spun around the apartment with the biggest *Shove It Up Your Keister* grin I've ever seen sporting the knee-high, fur-lined boots.

The combination of a brother's stubbornness and a mother's love yielded the kid *two* pairs of shoes.

Sigh.
God love Mom. She just wanted her kids to be happy.

> Garden Hose Lesson Learned:
> Little girls with no ballet training whatsoever
> can bust out world-class pirouettes
> when properly motivated.

6

Brushes with the spirit world, aka WTF was *that?*

As a child, three movies made me afraid of the dark–and one made me afraid of the sky.

The first was the 1973 film, *The Exorcist*. I must have been six or seven years old since I remember watching it in Uncle Harold's living room in Myrtle Beach, South Carolina. Why Mom allowed her kids to watch Linda Blair hurl pea soup and curse like a mad sailor is a decent parenting question.

Another movie was the 1974 made-for-TV movie, *Killer Bees*. The movie basically promised that a couple billion African killer bees were buzzing their way to

America and there was nothing anyone could do about it. For years, I used to look up at the sky with dread.

The third was the 1971 movie, *The Omega Man*. This I watched in Hawaii meaning the year *had* to have been either 1976 or 1977, which meant I was either eight or nine. There must have been a Charlton Heston marathon going on since I was further scared (and scarred) by the 1973 futuristic horror film, *Soylent Green*.

[Charlton only barely made it up to me when he found his voice in the 1968 science fiction classic, *Planet of the Apes*. You know, the whole, "Take yer stinking paws off me ya damn dirty ape!" I close my eyes and see myself as a youngster with the one-armed fist pump.]

I mention these films because kids (at least *this* kid) *believed* this crap.

I *believed* that demonic possession existed.

I *believed* that killer bees were on their way to swarm the living bejesus out of me.

I was *afraid* that the dark brought out those freaky nocturnal albino mutants.

And I didn't want to be turned into *Soylent Green* (*'cause it's made outta peeeee-pullllllllllll!*).

As a ten-year-old I finally realized that horror movies are made for entertaining–exactly like comedies. So when we talked Mom into dropping us off at the Porter 3 Theater for John Carpenter's 1978 masterpiece, *Halloween*, I didn't go home that night afraid that Michael Myers was going to appear out of the closet with a 14-inch knife. (And, hey, he only went after his family and they lived in Illinois so Porterville, California seemed safe enough.)

For the next six years I lived in the merry realization that ghosts, goblins, Great White sharks with personal vendettas, and lunatics who wore Captain Kirk masks were confined to the big screen at the Porter 3. Hell, we even cheered for the murderous ball in *Phantasm*, laughed at the dumbasses at Camp Crystal Lake running from the schmo in the hockey mask, and felt bad for poor Jack Nicholson holed up in that musty old hotel with that musty old Shelley Duvall.

And then, on three average nights in 1984, three events changed my perspective. They weren't *bumps in the night* since the freakiness happened right before my very eyes in our three-bedroom apartment in Porterville, California.

Incident #1: The Haunted Glass

David and I were sitting at our K-Mart-like dinette table. The kind with wobbly metal legs and a hard laminate surface. Give us a break, we were poor.

I can't remember why we were sitting there like a couple of mooks but, there we were. A glass of ice water sat between us. We were probably talking about girls.

On its own accord, the glass slid four inches across the table leaving a trail of water in its wake.

We looked at the glass then at each other.

"Did you see that?" David gasped.

With pounding heartbeat, I nodded.

The next day at school my Social Science teacher, Mr. Hevener, overheard the animated report to my friends and dismissed the whole thing.

"Those kinds of things happen all the time," he said.
They did?
He said either the table wasn't level or David pulled a fast one on me. I wasn't buying either explanation.

Incident #2: The Haunted Pitcher

Same brother. Same general area of the apartment.

We had an addiction to cheap grape juice and since David killed the last of it, he was obligated to make a fresh batch. The beige, hard plastic gallon-size Tupperware pitcher was our vessel of choice. To further add to *That Which Cannot Be Explained*, the light in the tiny kitchen was off but the light in the adjoining dining area was on.

There I sat at the crappy dinette table talking to him. Probably about girls.

He dumped the frozen concentrate into the pitcher, filled the pitcher in the sink, stirred the contents and sat the pitcher on the small crappy kitchen counter.

There he stood.

There I sat.

With our conversation at a proper stopping point– there were only so many times I could tell him how cute I thought Betsy was–he moved to put the pitcher away.

He grabbed it by the handle and lifted . . .

And dumped the entire gallon of grape juice on the linoleum floor.

"What are you doing?" I screamed.

I jumped up and flipped the kitchen light on. There he stood in shock, the now-empty pitcher still in his hands.

It was as if the pitcher had no bottom.

We cleaned up the pool of purple mess and examined the vessel.

It was perfectly intact.

And, no, he hadn't poured it out from the top. The thing just gave way *from the bottom* when he lifted it in front of my very eyes. We have never been able to explain it. And we continued to use that pitcher for years so, *weird.*

Really weird.

Incident #3: The Haunted Lamp

When it came time to actually *try* to reach out to the spirit world, David was clever enough to use *my* room for the exercise. Whatta guy. He brought in the Scrabble board and an air of determination. My small bedside lamp was the only source of illumination.

[And, up until that evening, I loved that little lamp. The base was one half of a coconut with two little hula figures perched between the miniature tree that held the light bulb. It was a cheap, Hawaiian touristy thing you could get in the Honolulu airport but it was *mine*.]

"Clear your mind," he said.

I laughed.

"Clear your mind and, without thinking, choose twenty letters."

"Whatever."

"Shh! Clear your mind and choose the letters that will spell out a message *from the dead*." He whispered these last three words. A flair for the dramatic? Yes, yes it was.

I did as instructed and we looked at the randomly chosen letters.

The room was suddenly very still.

My Contactor of the Dead brother whispered, "If anyone is there *give us a sign*."

At that *exact* moment, my kitschy Hawaiian lamp did something it had never done before.

It started flickering.

Off.

On.

Off.

On.

Off.

On.

We stared at each other until our eyebrows couldn't stretch any higher.

I gasped, "I'm getting the hell outta . . ."

"Shh! No! We have a message here in the letters!"

"The hell we do! I'm getting the hell outta here!"

I ran out of the room and two seconds later he joined me.

"What the hell was that?" I asked.

"We have to get back in there!"

"The hell we do! Thanks for inviting a ghost into *my* room!"

I didn't have the stones to play his little game again but the lamp ended up in the dumpster *that very night*.

All three of these unexplained phenomena happened my sophomore year in high school and, thus, in 1984, I became a believer that there are simply things that cannot be explained.

Now, *who you gonna call?*

> Garden Hose Lesson Learned:
> Some things you're not going to be able to explain.
> Live with it.

7

Eighties outtakes

I read quite a bit about *how* to write while I was penning my memoir; so much so that, many nights, my right hand typed away on the keyboard while my left hand held any number of Professor William Zinsser's books.

I also read the immeasurably helpful *On Writing: A Memoir of the Craft,* not that Stephen King needs the plug but, hey, I gotta give props where props are due. I'm still a little pissed at him for the dreadful *From a Buick 8* but he recovered nicely with *11/22/63: A Novel*.

In one of these How-To-Write books, the exact one escapes me, the message was this: *Don't just lead your reader around like a drunk at a party saying 'then I did this, then this, and then, for good measure, this.'*

There's also a writing equation that goes: *Write until you're done, put it a drawer for two weeks, then come back and cut 20%.*

Slaying your children, as Master King puts it (words, that is), *isn't* easy.

Writers love their words.

Like a dotting parent, we *protect and defend* our words.

We don't *want* to slay, but if we're smart, we listen to a guy who has sold more than 350 million books. That's 350 with *six* zeros behind it. That's *a lotta* books!

So I followed the Master's instructions and sliced and diced my beautiful tykes.

Oh, the pain!

And just as Master King resurrected the kid in *Pet Sematary*, I am sharing a few of *my* phoenixes now risen from the ashes. But unlike Stephen King's wicked creations, my resurrection won't keep you up at night.

[I was living on Mike's couch when I read *Pet Sematary*. Gage's return from the grave scared the living hell out of me and I kept waiting for that freaky little dead kid to rush me from the dark hallway.]

(Note: If you haven't read my *Eighties* memoir, now would be a *great* time! If you have no intention of reading it, you have my blessing to skip this chapter. If you're a Constant Reader, well, *read on!)*

• • •

Without a doubt, the school year 1985-1986 was one of the best years of my life. As I worked on balancing the content of the *Eighties* memoir, it was this time period that was the hardest to finish.

Not that I couldn't think of things to say. I had *too much* to say.

And so my friends, let us now return to the memories of my senior year of high school. I'll be judicial and limit it to three of my favorite recollections.

• • •

His name was Niki–an exchange student from Japan. Talk about *fearless*. How a kid finds himself in a small California town 5,000 miles from home is *impressive!*

Niki was magnetic. His personality, energy, and charm made him one of the most popular kids on campus. He spoke broken English, *loved* Madonna (and her CD at the time, *True Blue*), and wore neon-colored socks of pink and yellow.

People clamored to him.

I was one of those people.

We took Niki cruising with us every Friday and Saturday night. As part of the ritual, we'd end up at McDonald's and this is where we had the most fun with him.

He'd speak rapidly in Japanese, his hands flying all over the place; we'd listen intently then *translate*.

"Lalalalalalala."

"Uh huh, yeah. He wants a Big Mac."

"Blahblahblahblahblah."

"Large fries."

"Yayayayayaya."

"And a large Coke."

The cashier, in her burnt orange, skin tight polyester uniform looked at us in amazement. *We were actually translating Japanese!*

No, we weren't.

We knew what he wanted but, oh, it was funny. I guess you had to have been there.

God love you, Niki, wherever you are!

• • •

In addition to taking three Honors classes and pulling down a 4.3 grade point average; in addition to working at Longs Drugs after school and on the weekends; in addition to organizing rallies and attending school board meetings as School Board Representative on the student council.

I took a class at Porterville Junior College.

What possessed me to take the three-unit course, *Introduction to the Administration of Justice,* at that particular time–well, I have no explanation other than to say it was *divine intervention.*

Taking a college class as a high school kid, back then at least, required approval from the high school principal himself. I'm sure I had a reason (and it must have been a good one) because he granted me special dispensation to take the class.

Oh, I was a good college student too!

Sat in the front every time.

Actually read the $80 textbook.

Raised my hand and asked pertinent questions.

The college kids glared at me most evenings.

You could say I was eager. *Too* eager one night from the perspective of our instructor, a retired Deputy Sheriff.

"The Attica prison riot was a defining moment in the history of prisons in this country."

From my front row seat, I rubbed my right eye.

Our instructor scanned the room and continued.

"The year was 1971 and . . ."

I blinked and blinked again.

He stopped mid-sentence.

I blinked again.

I looked up at him, hoping I had rubbed out whatever was irritating my eye. *Was it an eyelash? Damn!*

He looked at me–his eyebrows narrowed–he struggled to continue.

"Attica . . . yeah . . . um . . . the riot . . ."

I sat upright as I realized that I wasn't blinking at him, I was *winking* at him. Both eyes shot open and I shook my head trying to communicate, *No! I wasn't hitting on you! Honest to God! No!* But it was too late; he gravitated to the other side of the room and never looked at me again for the entire semester.

Convinced I had studied hard enough for an A in the class, I ended up with a B but didn't have the stones to question him. I think I know the answer, though, and it had to do with an ill-timed eyelash from the eager-to-please high school kid.

[Note: I had no real reason for taking the class at that time. Four and a half years later, I had miscalculated my units to graduate from Cal State Northridge. Even with 3 units of summer school and 17 units of upper-division History classes (12 was considered full-time) my last semester, I was *still* 3 units short. But wait, I have 3 units of college credit from Porterville Junior College from 1986! *Brilliant!*]

• • •

And then there's the '86 Prom. The dance of all dances; the social event of all social events; *the last hurrah of high school.*

"So, I hear you want to borrow my Cadillac?" Mike's dad, Deke, asked.

"You heard correct," I smiled back. "We're thinking of a triple date and the Caddie is just the ticket. We'll *try* not to wreck it."

Mike said nothing but looked at the ground in an effort to hide his grin.

Mike's dad was built like a fireplug. Short and stocky with huge Popeye arms and a buzz cut, our fear of the man rivaled our respect for him. Not that Deke was abusive; he wasn't. He was just a hard-working blue-collar guy who rarely showed feelings of affection.

Deke looked at me and smiled. "'Course you can have the Caddie for a night. Just don't make me regret it."

"'Course *not*," I replied.

The big night arrived and the yellow Caddie gleamed a golden hue, spotless and ready for the triple date that was Kellie and I, Vicky and Mike, and Linda and Frank.

In a bit of irony, I had finally secured my date with that elusive varsity cheerleader–but Kellie and I were just friends. Not that that was a bad thing.

Having use of the long yellow, two-door El Dorado was not going to waste so we road-tripped 30 miles to Visalia for dinner. Bartles and Jaymes (the "Original" flavor) and California Coolers (with their sickly-greenish hue and bits of floating citrus) flowed freely between us.

Nowadays it seems, high schoolers are content with going through the drive-through at McDonald's for their Prom dinner but this was not the case in May, 1986. We settled for nothing less than the swanky Cask 'n Cleaver restaurant.

We laughed and conversed over our overpriced meals–meals that the guys were buying–chivalry was alive and well. Another couple from Monache had made the drive over and we raised our soda glasses to them across the crowded room. They were underclassmen but, no matter, we had concluded that age difference (all of one year at the most) was meaningless at that point. They were busy chatting with an old guy having dinner by his lonesome and we respected them all the more.

[When that couple went to pay their bill, they were told that the old man–who hadn't gone to his own Prom back in the day–had paid for their meal on his way out. Now *that's* memorable.]

We arrived at the Monache cafeteria more or less on time, the excitement of our grand entrance and the fruity wine coolers buzzing in our systems.

Kellie and I danced with our favorite teachers.

We danced with each other.

We danced with anyone who wanted to dance with us.

The music was loud, the cafeteria was packed, and our precious nine months as high school seniors was coming to its swift conclusion.

But the night was young.

After dancing to the very last song (without question a slow song but I don't recall what it was–I'd like to think it was Lionel Richie's *Say You, Say Me*, but that's just the 45-year-old talking), I suggested we continue the evening at the lake. Lake Success to be exact–roughly ten miles up the road–just the place to keep the party rolling. And what party is complete without alcohol? In my white tuxedo with sequined cummerbund and bow tie, I strolled into the Joy Jug liquor store.

[If you read *The Eighties*, you already know that the East Indian guy at the Joy Jug sold alcohol to anyone. The tuxedo *must* have been a dead giveaway that it was Prom Night in our little town but he simply didn't care that I was a minor.

OK, I do have a confession. I sorta knew the guy on an informal basis.

He used to buy cases of soda when Longs Drugs ran loss-leader ads. And there was no doubt he was simply going to resell the soda for a profit at his small liquor store, so he wasn't about to deny me the cheap champagne.]

While I was in the store, the girls threw away the empty wine cooler bottles that were piled up and rattling around the floorboard. This simple act would later prove *very significant.*

Upon exiting the store, my cohorts in the Caddie gave me a loud applause and away we went east along Highway 190.

It was quite dark that night and, had I paid closer attention in Mr. Forrest's Physical Science class, I probably could tell you if we were under a Waxing or Waning Gibbous or Crescent. But since the class was four years earlier and I earned an unimpressive D, I can't tell you anything about the phases of the moon that night.

Kellie and I grabbed our unopened bottle and made a run down the small hill to the dark shoreline. As Mike looked to park between the lines of the vacant parking lot (he was, after all, voted "Nicest" by our graduating class), the blackness was lit up like a Christmas tree.

"Put your hands where I can see them!" the Deputy barked through his loudspeaker. Oh, this did *not* look good.

Mike, the golden boy in his own spotless white tuxedo, shot his hands up in the air like he was being robbed at gunpoint.

Kellie and I crouched in the darkness, our hearts slamming in our chests.

"What are we going to do if they get arrested?" she whispered.

To this I had no answer but I was thinking, *What if he rats us out down here?*

In retrospect, it would have been pretty silly to slap the cuffs on two couples in formal Prom attire. After all, the alcohol *wasn't* yet opened so it wasn't like the two trembling couples were breaking any laws.

[Actually, *minor in possession* is a misdemeanor but, again, *it was freaking Prom Night!*]

Now had the Deputy found a *dozen* empty wine coolers on the floor, the night could have ended quite differently. Most likely with Kellie and I abandoning our bottle and scrambling back up the embankment to join the ranks of the *busted*.

Glug, glug, glug.

There goes the cheap Asti Spumante!

Blah, blah, blah, blah, blaaaaaah.

The sound of the Deputy, complete with finger extended into Mike's white ruffles, giving Mike the, "You're lucky I'm in a good mood. Now you get these good girls home now Mister!" With the coast clear and the lurking Deputy moving onto the next Prom couple cruising along the dirt road behind us, Kellie and I rejoined the group.

"Hahaha! Mike! *Busted!*"

"Shut up, Tom! This is not funny!" Mike snapped. "We almost got arrested!"

"Ah, lighten up Francis! Hey, Kellie and I will share our bottle!"

"Do *not* open that bottle in this car!"

We drove back to town but the mood had soured considerably.

> Garden Hose Lesson Learned:
> Share the stories of *your* growing up years!
> Someone, somewhere will benefit from them.

8

Ode to Odie: Don't sweat the small stuff, just load the wagon!

My first impression of Odie Dewayne Miller was that I didn't like the guy.

In the ultimate display of *It's Not What You Know, It's Who You Know*, I walked into the hospital maintenance shop *dressed* as a hospital maintenance man: gray work pants, new work boots and freshly-ironed blue work shirt–all spotless and wrinkle-free. It was 6:15 a.m. and, though I was fifteen minutes early, I was the last of the Day Shift Blue Collars waiting to punch the clock. You see, the fellas knew I was coming and weren't about to miss the arrival of their wide-eyed new co-worker.

Don't Fight with the Garden Hose

Never mind that I knew *absolutely nothing* about maintaining *anything*, I got the job through association (boyfriend of the Administrator's daughter) and, hey, as they said in that Johnny Bravo episode of The Brady Bunch, *The suit fit*.

I walked through the door and promptly leaned against a work bench like I owned the damn place.

Steve, Wayne and Bill looked at the floor.

Paul nodded and turned away.

Al lit a cigarette and blew smoke at the ceiling.

Odie stared. And grinned. And stared some more.

The three Night Shift guys came straggling in amidst quiet mumblings of *this is bullshit* and *what a bunch of horseshit!* It's possible they threw in other expressions of farm animal excrement but I was *trying* to ignore them. Hell, I was *trying* to blend in.

For five of the longest minutes of my life, the Cold Shoulder Reception raged.

With the small shop at maximum capacity–the intersection of the two shifts at the time clock–Odie finally broke his silence.

"So, we hear you're the Administrator's nephew!"

What a jerk off.

"You heard wrong."

By the end of the first day, the two Day Shift Supervisors were convinced that Odie and I hated each other so the next day we were partnered up–*for the rest of the summer*. The two bosses wanted me gone as badly as the entire crew and figured this was a good start toward my accelerated resignation.

What the bosses failed to recognize was that Odie and I hit it off away from the rest of the fellas.

He was ten years older than me and the guy had seen his share of life experience. Left to father two young children after his wife died of breast cancer, he remarried and became a step-father to another child. Via daylong discussions comfortably nestled in the privacy of a junction of air-conditioning ducts, he told me how *wonderful* his life was and his undying love of God.

In the days before manning the Day Shift with walkie-talkies, once Odie and I disappeared into the ceiling–in our cool and pitch-black hiding place–we were *off the grid* until we reappeared for lunch loudly bitching about how much we hated each other.

I told him how tough college was. All that studying! Dating multiple girls! You know, real challenging stuff like going to the gym at 11:00 p.m.

"Don't sweat the small stuff," he'd say, "just load the wagon!"

We had *a ball* the summer of '89.

We played on the company softball team.

We played cards on the weekend.

We saw *Total Recall* and got totally hammered afterward, loudly picking apart the story line at a local bar.

We *tried* to serve divorce papers on an ER nurse's husband only to be quickly surrounded by the guy's redneck friends smacking pipes and wrenches in their palms. We ended up getting chased back to my VW Scirocco *nearly* getting our asses stomped. Oh, we laughed about that afterward.

We peeled out at the Wendy's drive-through after the guy gave us two enormous sacks of food after we had only ordered two bucks worth!

Yeah, we had a ball together.

Then suddenly the summer was over and I returned to Cal State Northridge for my senior year. Odie left the hospital and enrolled in the police academy and I only saw him occasionally.

One day his son, Scotty Dewayne, aka *Scotty Do-Dane* aka, *The Do-Daner*, fell off his bike. Resulting tests showed a malignant brain tumor and, within months, Odie's young boy slipped away on the living room couch. He was only 7 years old.

Odie disenrolled from classes during this overwhelmingly stressful time and, sadly, his second marriage didn't survive the loss of the child.

But Odie's faith never waned.

"Don't sweat the small stuff . . ." (even though this was *seriously big* stuff.)

After losing his wife; after losing his young son; after managing through a divorce; Odie's faith never waned.

". . . just load the wagon!"

He left Porterville for his home state of Texas and I lost track of him completely.

Sigh.

Years passed.

The phone rang on the evening of December 12, 2001.

"Hello?"

"Tom, this is Meg." (My ex-girlfriend from Porterville.)

"*Meg?* Hi, how are you?"

"I don't mean to disturb you but I have news you need to hear."

"Um, yeah?"

"Odie's been in an accident this morning. He's in a Texas hospital and they don't think he's going to make it. Stephanie is expecting your call in the ICU waiting room."

"Oh my God."

When I spoke to Odie's daughter, Stephanie, that evening, I was ready to catch the first plane to Killeen but she instructed me to stay put. The prognosis was grim and there was simply nothing anyone could do.

Good Samaritan Odie had stopped to help a lady in the thick Harker Heights fog only to get creamed by a car in the near-whiteout conditions. With a severed spine and shattered bones, he spent five days swimming in fire and shadows–comatose and with a near-fatal fever–looking for a way out of the fiery blackness. Dozens of people streamed in to see his broken body, all convinced this was their last good-bye. He recounted to me later that he heard the voices around him, including, "He's not going to make it," and, "This guy is *seriously* mangled." He prayed his way out of the darkness and, when the fever broke, he opened his eyes to a new reality.

You would think that being paralyzed from the chest down meant an absence of pain but, sadly, this wasn't the case. His teeth were shattered, his legs were broken, his spine was severed but he felt pain *everywhere*. Where he supposedly couldn't feel anything, his muscles spasmed uncontrollably. I'm no clinician but when a body is traumatized beyond recovery, it simply doesn't know what to do to repair itself.

Odie would eventually be discharged and live with his sister and her family.

[No million dollar settlements here as the lady he was trying to help and the guy that crushed him in the street were both uninsured. Perfect.]

He developed what I call an *X-Box Existence*.

I'd send him the latest game and, for those that met his enthusiastic approval, I'd buy a copy for myself so we could play online together. His favorites included *Rainbow Six Vegas 1 & 2*, *Borderlands*, *Call of Duty 4: Modern Warfare*, *Battlefield: Bad Company*, *Earth Defense Force 2017* and *Mercenaries 2: World in Flames*.

Each of these games allowed him to temporarily escape the reality of a T-6 paraplegic. With his surround-sound headphones on, he immersed himself into a world where he ran freely in the mud and blood–hurling himself forward, leading the charge, shouting words of encouragement to other online gamers, *often times getting himself splattered in the process*. I often snuck out of work early to join him on the battlefield.

One of the funniest moments came in the middle of the night while he and I were playing a game called *Left 4 Dead*. The game throws four online gamers into the fray of a zombie-killing apocalypse. The lone female character, Zoey, was his character of choice. In fact, he loved games where the main character was female (*Velvet Assassin* and *Tomb Raider: Underground* come to mind). He'd exclaim, "She's cuter than a bug's ear! Why would I want to look at a guy all day long?"

One of the aberrations in *Left 4 Dead* has a lethal 20-foot projectile tongue. Once he nails you with it, there is *nothing* you can do other than watch yourself get dragged back to meet your doom of gnashing monster teeth. Zoey, I mean, *Odie*, found himself in the *tongue clutch* this particular evening.

"Help me! Help me! Help me!" he screamed into his headset.

"Nothing I can do! Nothing I can do! Nothing I can do!"

Odie's brother-in-law stormed into the room.

"What in *the* hell is going on here? It's 2 a.m.! I thought you fell out of bed!"

Left 4 Dead, as far as I know, was the only game officially banned in his house.

When he wasn't in front of the TV battling it out on X-Box Live, he could be found zipping his electric wheelchair over to the nearest Mini-Mart for munchies. I supplemented his diet every time I went to Costco, (chewy pepperoni sticks and soft turkey jerky were the go-to staples) and enjoyed sending him things as much as he enjoyed receiving them.

But he constantly struggled with his injuries–an open sore on his ankle that never healed and pressure sores on his legs and buttocks. His home-health nurse, a gal he called *Jo-Jo* (her name must have been Jolene or Jody or something along those lines), tried her best to keep him healthy but it was a losing battle. I asked him one day why they wouldn't just lop his legs off and get rid of all that dead weight. He said that his body wouldn't know how to heal itself after such a major surgery.

Twice that I recall, his condition warranted admission into the hospital and the VA in Dallas was where he received the bulk of his care.

[His stint in the Army as a Tent Repair Specialist afforded him access to Veteran's services. Thank God for that.]

Oh, he did *not* look forward to the sweaty, bumpy 3-hour transport from Abilene to Dallas. His stays were longer than expected–literally months at a time–but he tried to keep a positive outlook. He brought the X-Box but couldn't access the internet–the Dallas VA wi-fi must have been non-existent at the time–meaning he couldn't connect to the outside world.

My brother, Lorne, and I kept the care packages flowing–Lorne even had a pizza delivered to the VA making Odie an instant celebrity with everyone on his floor. I carefully hid a can of Coors Light in one of his care packages, under the packets of beef jerky and Slim Jims, (he loved it in the bottle but I was too afraid it'd get broken in transit) and we planned and plotted how he'd:

1) open the package without getting busted,
2) stash the can without getting busted,
3) get it cold without getting busted, and
4) how he'd ultimately drink it without getting busted.

This digression broke up some of the monotony and he found an ally in one of his regular nurses who aided and abetted our endeavor. Odie ended up sharing his lone can of beer with his roommate. What a guy!

While he became wistful at times, recounting the days when he'd take the love of his life, Michelle, dancing until they closed the place down; later when he'd buzz her and the kids in his homemade ultra-light airplane; when Michelle died in his arms in the very hospital he and I worked together; when Scotty took his last breath on the living room couch; he never once felt sorry for himself. He never once cursed God.

Not once.

"Don't sweat the small stuff, Tom," he'd say. Everything in this short life was *the small stuff* in his eyes.

I last spoke to him on December 10, 2009 on my cell phone. He had been in the local Abilene hospital for weeks and his voice was no more than a whisper.

"Are you going to make it out of there Odie?" I asked. I couldn't believe how weak he sounded.

"I sure hope so."

Eventually, I said my usual goodbye.

"I love you, brother."

"I love you too, Tom."

Those were the last words he spoke to me. In the early hours of December 12, Odie's sister called. It was Saturday morning so I listened to the message around 9 a.m.

"Dewayne passed away this morning, Tom. I thought you should know. He loved you very much. Thank you for all that you did."

Her teary message felt like a sledge-hammer to the stomach and I sat down in the walk-in closet sobbing uncontrollably. After a few minutes I emerged and cried in Susan's arms. My best friend, my inspiration, was gone. Through all his hardship Odie used to tell me that, while he didn't *want* to die, he *did* look forward to his reunion with Michelle and Scotty. He came to me in my dreams that evening, grinning from ear to ear with this simple message:

You should see what kind of deal I have now!

I woke up in tears but knew, deep down, Odie was finally at peace; no longer a prisoner to his broken body.

• • •

I flew into the Dallas Fort Worth airport and picked up a guy I'd never met at Love Field. Ken flew in from Orlando–a gamer who, along with his wife, had fought many online battles with us. We drove the 150 miles to Killeen–crying and laughing until it hurt–recounting the times Odie led us into battle.

At the funeral Ken did a colorful impersonation of Odie:

"I may be paralyzed from my titties down, but that's not going to slow me down!" I looked around and cringed at the use of the word *titties* in church.

I recounted the story when Odie sang *Happy Birthday* to my girlfriend in the middle of a quiet and expensive restaurant. At the appointed time, he burst in with his handlebar mustache, bolo tie and cowboy boots, singing:

"Happy birthday to yoooou. Happy birthday toooo ew-ew-ew-ew youuuuuuuuuu."

His version was twangy, obnoxious, painfully slow, and unforgettable. He finished to rousing applause and enjoyed as many free drinks as he wanted at the bar before leaving.

I'm not worried about my friend these days.

And I am glad he's not hurting.

But I miss him every day.

He's not far away, though. Multiple times a day, I hear his voice clearly in my mind:

"Don't sweat the small stuff, Tom. Just load the wagon!"

I'm trying, my friend. I'm trying.

Odie with the love of his life, Michelle

Garden Hose Lesson Learned:
If you think your life blows and you're feeling
sorry for yourself, there's ALWAYS
someone who has it worse
who's loving every minute of it!

8 (a)

Odie in the Kill Zone

[Excerpt from an email from Odie to me, January 10, 2008. FYI, he is describing the *Call of Duty 4* map known as "Bloc," a map notorious for snipers. This is all Odie–I've not edited it in any way.]

I lost my companion last night!
It was 0200 in the morning. I had my sights on this really nasty terrorist. He killed three of my men as they pushed to capture Objective Charley. We survived a heavy barrage from an enemy airstrike and the young men under my command were reluctant to venture out from the safety of our covered position. But every one of my guys were Recon Rangers. With blood and sweat in their eyes, they raced down the open alley way of blown out buildings and burned up cars. I helplessly watched

the young men die before they could make it to the nearest cover. A sniper, one with deadly precision, was racking up the kills.

I couldn't send another soldier to his death, so I took it upon myself to be the next man to make the run. I launched from cover out into full view of the offending opponent, but what I lacked in speed I made up for in experience. Before the sniper could get a lock on me I dove behind a small pile of busted cinderblocks; while lying perfectly still as the marksman hammered at my cover. The rock fragments and flying dirt stung my face and hands as the bullets whizzed within inches of my body. After a short while, the terrorist, figuring he had killed me, started searching through his scope for another easy kill.

I carefully took the 50 caliber sniper rifle off my back. Cradling it through one of the cinderblocks, I slowly scanned the far side of the battle ground for any sign of the invisible assailant. His camouflage was top grade. He probably spent morning hours replenishing the grass and shrubs on his Gilly suit.

Pop! Out of the corner of my scope, a muzzle flash. Another one of my guys drops to the ground. THarvey had peeked his head around the corner of the building to look for the sniper and paid with his life. I dialed my scope in on the location of the flash. There he was, so well hidden that even with my Leupold 3.5-10x40 Mark 4 scope I could barely pick him out of the landscape. He looked to be right-handed, so aiming just three inches to the right of the barrel I see the shrub-covered hand posed to take another life.

Calculating the location of his temple, I squeeze off the shot. The ground beneath my powerful rifle rumbles and then the air becomes very still. I waved the next youngster out and down the alley. Then I stood up to follow and . . .

Everything goes black! I smell the burning stench of something on fire. I immediately thought, *Maybe I didn't get the sniper, maybe I'm in Hell, he may have still had enough left to take me out.* The screeching in my ears, the smell of something burning; I open my eyes and realize–the screeching is my own voice! The smell is my X-Box as it catches fire and the silicone inside burns! My *Call of Duty 4* game is now forever welded in the tray of my best companion I have ever known. All the screeching and yelling will not bring my friend back. It, like a virtual sniper bullet to the head of a virtual enemy, may never see the light of day again.

Now it's going to be long weeks before I get my X-Box back from Microsoft. Microsoft may not know the horror a gamer will suffer at the thought of sending his baby off for major reconstructive repairs. All I ask of you, my email friends, is your prayers. I will be losing my sanity during the long wait. Pray that I have the fortitude to stick this out and not go off the deep end with gaming withdrawals!

Your Brother in Christ, Odie

• • •

And so you now have the flavor of my fun loving friend, the late Odie Dewayne Miller.

Of course, I wasn't about to let him languish without an X-Box so, within a day, a new one was speeding its way to Abilene, Texas. I also sent him a new copy of

Call of Duty 4 since his was permanently fused inside his melted machine–and from there, the battles began anew!

Odie in happier times

> Garden Hose Lesson Learned:
> Getting your melon splattered online
> just might be the highlight of another guy's day . . .
> so give him a break!

9

Stars walk among us

Stepping back to the days of 1997 and my first experience living in Seattle, I paid close attention to the big city concert scene. And I saw some big bands in small venues (The Tubes and Missing Persons at The Ballard Firehouse, Loverboy at Parker's Casino, Berlin and The Church at The Fenix Underground). When I saw that Fleetwood Mac was coming to the Tacoma Dome, I decided that I didn't want to do it solo. Fleetwood Mac, one of those classic, *timeless* bands worthy of sharing. Worthy of flying someone up from the old hometown.

I picked up the phone and asked Shawnie if she wanted to come up from Porterville. It took all of five seconds before the enthusiastic, breathless, "Yes! I love Lindsay Buckingham! Oh, I can't wait!"

• • •

Shawnie and I have enjoyed a mutual adoration since the first time I laid eyes on her. There, at her freshman walk-around day in 1985, she was *clearly in a daze.* Amidst the swirl of three hundred soon-to-be freshmen racing to sign up for classes filling up fast, there she stood paralyzed on system overload. I made a beeline for her. As a soon-to-be senior and on the Student Council, I had volunteered to help the incoming students.

"Hi," I said, smiling at her.

"Hi," she said miserably.

"Can I help you with your schedule today?"

"Yes. *Please!*"

From that day on we were the best of friends. And while she was–and is–a total knock-out babe, she's always been like a little sister to me.

• • •

Different combinations of people have surrounded drummer Mick Fleetwood to make up Fleetwood Mac over the years. I had a vague notion that Stevie Nicks was in there but didn't know any of the other people. Shawnie would bring me up to speed the weekend she came up.

Like any good Seattleite with an out-of-town guest, we rode the Monorail to the Space Needle and looked out over Seattle and Puget Sound. We toured Pike Place Market and indulged in deep-fried mini-doughnuts (where the grease saturated the bottom of the paper sack). Yeah, fun times downtown!

With one eye on the flying fish and the other on my watch, it was time to make our way back to the car to prepare for the concert at the Tacoma Dome that night. We began climbing University Street to the parking garage.

When we happened along the Fairmont Olympic Hotel, we stopped to look at the unusual scene: a dozen guys–not a single girl–excitedly huddled on the sidewalk. The one common thing between them–besides the beards and long hair–was their Fleetwood Mac albums and Sharpies.

No way. No way do I have this kind of luck.

"What's going on?" I asked Bearded Guy #1.

"We're trying to get Mick's autograph. Don't you know Fleetwood Mac's playing the Tacoma Dome tonight?"

I looked at Shawnie in disbelief.

"Actually we have tickets and are going there now! You saying Mick Fleetwood's staying at this hotel?"

The guy looked at me with the expression, *Are you a total moron?*

"The entire band is staying here!"

Looking at the dozen other eager album clutchers this had to be the truth, or these guys were all misinformed. And so we joined them. They didn't seem to mind we were album less; after all, a pretty young brunette *girl* had joined the ranks.

Twenty minutes passed as the bearded fellas debated the merits of the various albums in their possession. I was partial to the 1982 album, Mirage, and offered up that my friend Sherman and I used to cruise to the cowbell clatter of *Hold Me*. This elicited frowns so I quickly offered up that I thought the song with the USC marching band was "pretty bitchen." Heads nodded as the merits of *Tusk* were debated.

And sure as hell, a black limo pulled up to the curb and John McVie walked out the front door, cut through the throng of dudes and dove in the waiting car. No autographs from the bass guitarist but no one really seemed to mind.

Five minutes later, keyboardist Christine McVie did the exact same thing. Shawnie's excitement was building–and this confused me–since I thought Lindsey was female (and must have been Christine) and Christine had just blown us off.

Stevie Nicks' appearance got the group really excited but she, too, wasn't in the autograph mood and sped past the group into limo #3.

Not sure who actually made up the band, I thought we were down to Mick himself, but with Shawnie hopping up and down, I thought, *Mick is the old, long-haired hippy looking dude. Is she really that excited to see Mick Fleetwood?*

"Here comes Lindsey!" she squealed and a guy that looked like a bona fide rock star–thin with long hair and brown leather pants–appeared at the front door. Like the three band mates before him, he zipped through the guys into black limo #4.

It must be written in a Groupie Etiquette manual somewhere that once a rock star enters a limo–with pitch black window tint–they are no longer physically present. As soon as Lindsey dove into the limo, all attention turned back to the front door and the soon-to-appear leader of the band. But the limo just sat there. *Lindsey's still here! Lindsey's a dude! I brought the only girl to this shindig!*

Shawnie looked at the limo and back to me. I stepped forward and whispered in her ear, "Tap on the window and see what happens."

Tap, tap, tap.

Whirrrrrrrrrrrrrrrrrrr.

Suddenly she was half in the car, draped over the door at her waist, her butt in the air and her shoes four feet off the ground. After about a minute, she extracted herself from this horizontal position, the window flew up and Lindsey's limo sped off.

"Well? What did he say? Did you score us backstage passes? Tell me!" I asked excitedly. To this day, the only response has been a dreamy smile. Did he kiss her? I have no idea.

Mick appeared on the threshold and was instantly surrounded by albums and Sharpies thrust in the air. After signing as many as he could in sixty seconds, Mick finally said, "Got to go to the show now."

But what he *actually* said was, "Got to go to the *shoe* now. Got to go to the *shoe*" in whatever accent that changes show to shoe. Good old Mick was born in Cornwall, England so it must be a United Kingdom thing. I loved the guy for taking the time to acknowledge the bearded groupies–a simple act that no one else had.

I find it interesting that the five members of Fleetwood Mac traveled to Tacoma in five separate limos. Could they not stand each other offstage? It is conceivable when you think that the McVie's were former spouses and it's pretty well believed that Lindsey and Stevie knew each other in the biblical sense. Hell, Mick might have been doing them all for all I know. Who knows what kind of stress rock stars endure on the road?

We drove to Tacoma and saw one of the best concerts I've ever seen. I fell in love with a song I'd never heard before that night, *Silver Springs*.

The traveling evangelist [as described in *The Eighties*] back in the day spewed that, "Everybody knows Stevie Nicks is a modern day witch who gets her power from Satan!" Images of candle-lit rooms with jeweled chalices full of blood and half-naked guys wearing goat heads come to mind–and Stevie presiding over this obscenity–with Ozzy Osbourne in a black cloak hurling raspberry jam. OK, never mind that image and what that moron preacher had to say about the evils of rock music and the source of Stevie Nicks' talent. The lady can flat out perform so I say *God bless her!*

And thanks to Lindsey for rolling down the window and making my friend's day. And night. And month.

> Garden Hose Lesson Learned:
> Stars walk among us!
> Just keep your expectations low
> because they might be going to a shoe
> or the loo, for that matter!

10

That the Paul David Hewson urinal?

P aul David Hewson (DOB: May 10, 1960), short of JC Himself, is arguably the coolest cat to walk the earth.

He's been granted an honorary knighthood by Queen Elizabeth II.

He's been nominated for the Nobel Peace Prize.

He rubs elbows with presidents and popes and billionaires.

He's one of the biggest humanitarian forces on the planet.

You may not know him as Paul, but you do know him as the lead singer of the biggest, baddest band on the planet: U2.

"Bah-No."

Not like the Bono of Sonny and Cher. The guy's *so cool* that the entire planet knows how to pronounce it correctly.

Admittedly, I didn't pay much attention to U2 prior to 1987's, The Joshua Tree, so can't claim to be a *true* U2 aficionado. And since I graduated in 1986, the Irish foursome just wasn't a part of the high school fabric.

My friend, Betsy, who I had a very serious *Notes In The Locker Relationship* way back when, holds firm that, "If you don't go back to Boy, you're not a *real* fan." Who am I to argue with *that?*

I did take notice of The Joshua Tree, just enough to include a few of their songs on a few of my college mixtapes. Let's just say the Irish fellas got my attention.

And then Rattle and Hum came along in 1988 and I *tried* to like it. I really did.

I tried to like Bono.

But I just couldn't do it.

With a mullet from hell and the jeans-tucked-in-the-cowboy-boots thing.

I. Just. Couldn't. Do. It.

I couldn't get past the look to hear the sound.

Bono was a Bad Ass and I didn't get it. To put it bluntly, he was *Way Too Cool Way Too Soon* for me.

Years passed. Sometimes it takes me awhile to come around. Sometimes it takes a new millennium.

Enter my friend Stephen and All That You Can't Leave Behind.

I met Stephen my first night of grad school in 1990 at Cal State Bakersfield. Our instructor embarrassed me by proclaiming that, "In addition to class studies, each of you will need to find an internship like Tom Harvey here in the front row."

She pointed at me and I immediately felt the burning eyes of twenty students boring a hole in the back of my head. After class, a guy sporting leopard-print Thomas Dolby-esque glasses and a doo reminiscent of the lead singer of Flock of Seagulls walked up to me.

"So," he demanded, "how did *you* get an internship already?"

His expression was way too serious (a look, I soon discovered, he acquired from his Pre-Med days at UC Davis).

"You look like a Depeche Mode fan."

He smiled.

"As a matter of fact I am."

And that was our first interaction.

Over the next two years, we finished our Masters Degrees and went down the path of marriage, mortgages, and the pursuit of fun when we weren't poring over spreadsheets and wearing overpriced ties.

The year was suddenly 2000 and, *hey*, we all survived the Y2K bug. The phone rang, area code 619, meaning one thing: Stephen checking in.

"Whassup bro?"

"Ever seen U2 live?"

"Nope."

"I just scored four tickets in Las Vegas. Seeing U2 live is like going to church. We're going."

"Like going to church? What does that mean?"

"It's a spiritual experience. You'll see."

Out strutted Bono to a sold-out crowd at the Thomas and Mack Arena and, let me tell you, I've *never* seen such confidence. I thought I knew something about live music but U2 *redefined* the concert experience. Bono strutted out to *Elevation* and proceeded to take the capacity crowd (19,522 according to Wikipedia) to the First Church of Rock 'N Roll. Holy moly, were Elvis still alive, I'm certain the King would have been in the front row rocking the one-armed fist pump.

So now that we've established that Bono rubs elbows with billionaires, and the one who founded Microsoft lives a few neighborhoods away from Susan and me, *the sighting* peaked my interest.

Bono was spotted at the popular West Seattle restaurant, Salty's.

This caused me to reflect that maybe–just maybe– the *supercool* walk among us from time to time. With a beautiful view of Puget Sound and the downtown skyline, and some of the best seafood around, I could see Bono strutting through the front doors of Salty's sporting his *uber*cool Armani shades.

He may have enjoyed his fine dining in a corner booth overlooking the water.

He may have eaten downstairs for a private dining experience.

In either case, he *probably* used one of the two public restrooms, which caused me to reflect, *again*. So on my next trip to Salty's, I took inventory:

Three urinals, three stalls on the main level.

Three urinals, two stalls downstairs.

Noted.

I'm no mathematician but it only takes simple math to conclude that it would take a guy eleven trips to accomplish the obvious: to stand in the *exact* spot Bono stood; to go where Bono, uh, *went*.

Seriously, what 40-something guy wouldn't want to be shoulder to shoulder with Bono? What guy wouldn't say (without trying to look down), "Bono? My Irish brutha from another mutha! Let me buy you a pint!"

And, thus, my personal quest began.

It took me three years and six visits, but I covered all the variables. I believe, with a long, respectful sigh, that Bono and I have shared the same bathroom receptacle–and to him I say, *Thank you very much* for the near spiritual experiences in the Salty's crapper. Each one taken with care and a calm sense of humility, appreciation, and, dare I say, love?

Now the naysayers would say, *There's probably a private restroom and that's probably what he used!* To this I say, *Don't pee on my parade!* Bono doesn't *need* a private restroom. Bono mingles with the little people, *even* in the men's room.

And so my friends, I challenge you to keep an open mind and embrace this reality:

Fellas, the next time nature calls, you might just be shoulder to shoulder with a bonafide superstar. You may be in an airport or at a ballgame and the guy next to you might, *just might*, be Mick Fleetwood or Tom Cruise or Denzel Washington–or Bono himself.

Ladies, the stall next to you just might occupy Taylor Swift or Cameron Diaz or Charlize Theron.

Something to think about.

> Garden Hose Lesson Learned:
> Stars walk among us so
> they *must* pee among us.

1 1

The visit

My step-grandfather, Adam, and I were surprisingly close. For a guy with no shortage of kids (six sons and six daughters from his first wife, Helen), Grandpa's love and affection was in high demand.

[One son and one daughter died at childbirth so that left him with five of each sex. I could probably name eight of them if I had to.]

Looking back, it really was Cosmic Good Timing that in 1977 my grandma and her second husband were empty-nesters. When Mom's divorce proceedings began in Hawaii, Grandma and Grandpa suddenly had two more children to raise in Central California. The fact that they had raised fourteen kids between them made them experts at parenting. It was Parenting Round Two for them and they loved it.

I can't say exactly why *Grandpa* [there was no *step* about it] and I shared the bond we did. Maybe he felt sorry for me for being the youngest of the boys. Whatever the case, he made me feel like a favored son, so much so that some of his real kids were a bit flabbergasted.

David and I lived under their roof for two school years (4th and 5th grades for me, 1977-1978). When Mom finished her nursing studies, we moved six miles down the road from Terra Bella to Porterville.

My recollection of my grandparents after the 5th grade tends to lose focus. Oh, we got together for Christmases and birthdays, but as we grew into teenagers, David and I largely forgot about them. They were going to live forever, after all. They were always going to be there.

In 1982, Grandpa made the 6-mile drive to Porterville to watch me play football. He wore his usual blue jeans, long-sleeve cowboy shirt, bolo tie, and his sandy red hair poked out from under a Clark Forklift trucker hat. Standing next to the small bleachers with his big strong hands tucked into his pockets, he said to whomever would listen, "Number 21. He's mine." I gave him a quick wave from the sidelines and he nodded with a big grin. God, was he proud. It didn't matter that I *gave up* a couple touchdowns–worst cornerback in Monache freshman football history, I'm convinced–and we got our asses kicked that day. All that mattered was that I invited him and it was important to me. He came because that's what dads did.

In 1984, I made the 6-mile drive to Terra Bella in a borrowed Cadillac on Prom Night and proudly showed off my pretty blonde girlfriend, Lynn. I came because that's what sons did.

The memories are few and far between as the high school and college years flew by.

As the years passed, Grandma grew frail.

Our beautiful Greyhound, John, and Doberman, Killer, eventually disappeared.

It pains me to write these words.

It pains me to have tossed my grandparents aside like my old Winnie the Pooh. But, like Pooh Bear, my grandparents were never going to die. They would always be there when I needed to return to them. Always.

By the time I finished college and landed back in Porterville, they had moved to the dusty town of Tulare. Twenty five long miles away. Given the *long* distance, I rarely visited.

[To put *that* in perspective, I drive thirty five miles for work every day, one-way.]

And then the improbable happened.

In 1994, Grandma suffered a stroke sitting in her chair and seven long, exhausting days later, she passed away in the hospital as my 51-year-old mother wailed like a baby at her side. Though I was 26 at the time, watching Mom hold vigil at Grandma's bedside was surreal and confusing. Little did I know at the time that, *You only have one mother and age makes no difference when you know she's dying.* That was a lesson I wouldn't learn for another 14 years.

By this time, Grandpa's kids were grandparents themselves and scores of people, some I had never met, took turns staying with him around the clock. David and I, at our naïve best, thought that it was a great opportunity for him to start dating. Yeah, he and I suffer from *Shit-For-Brains-Itis* from time to time.

After Grandma died, Grandpa seldom spoke and seemed to be lost in a fog. Doctors call this Failure To Thrive but I wouldn't know *these* words for another 14 years when Mom spiraled into her own depression.

And then the impossible happened.

My strong-as-an-ox grandpa suddenly needed an oncologist. They said he had colon cancer but I knew he'd beat it. I visited him, once, in the summer of 1994 because, you know, that 25-mile drive was *such* an inconvenience.

The year became 1995 and I took a trip out to see how my de facto dad was conquering those two ugly words, *colon cancer*. I was not prepared for what I saw.

I rapped on the screen door and walked into the quiet house without waiting for a reply. A guy I had never met before, a husband of one of the five daughters, was watching TV in the dark.

"Oh, I'm Tom, a grandson. Is Grandpa here?"

He introduced himself–though I can't remember his name–and nodded to the adjacent bedroom. I strolled in the room expecting to see my 220-pound grandpa sitting in bed strumming his guitar. On the nightstand stood two framed pictures: Dirty Harry with that massive .44 magnum in his hand and Joe Montana, rolling out of the pocket, in his 49er glory days.

But the tiny form under the covers couldn't be my big, strong grandpa. This was a cruel joke. My heart started pounding in my chest and I quickly backed out of the room. Turning to the stranger in the living room, I asked, "Do you mind stepping outside for a few moments? I'd like to talk with him alone." Seeing the shock on my face, the son-in-law smiled sadly and walked out the front door without saying a word.

I tried swallowing the rising nausea in my throat–tried to put on a brave face–but it was hopeless.

"Hi Grandpa," I croaked, the tears streaming down my face.

The tiny figure opened his eyes and for a moment we just gazed at each other. His face was completely stripped away of its fullness but the cancer hadn't touched his bright blue eyes.

"Hi Son," he whispered.

I pulled up a chair and took his hands in mine. His once strong hands were now half the size of mine. These weren't his hands–these were the hands of a child.

"I should have come sooner. I'm so sorry I haven't been to see you."

"It's OK, Son."

"I like . . . your . . . pictures," I managed to say, the words broken by sobs.

"You know," he whispered, "I don't know who I like better, Clint Eastwood or John Wayne."

We both smiled.

"Hmm. I've never thought about that. That's a tough one."

"Son, I need to tell you something."

"Yeah, Grandpa?"

"If you're ever in trouble, go to Meredith or Terry for help." These were his oldest and youngest sons.

"OK, Grandpa."

I left the house that night and picked up the brick of a phone I had mounted in my car–the cell phone plan that allowed *ten* free minutes a month for $49.99–and at twenty five cents a minute thereafter, called David in Sacramento.

"Hello?"

"You need to get down here! I'm in Tulare and you need to get down here!" I yelled.

"Yeah, we'll get down there one of these days."

"NO!" I screamed, the tears blurring my vision. "He's dying! You need to come *right now!*" I was hysterical.

"OK, OK. Relax. Calm down!"

"Don't tell me to calm down!"

The next Saturday, Mom, David, and Tricia made the four hour drive from Sacramento and I met them in Tulare. There were fifty or more people crowded in the small house. Women cooked in the small kitchen. Men stood outside smoking and talking quietly. Kids played in the yard. Time was short and everyone knew it.

And there we were–four people with no blood relation to any of them–four people tied to my step-grandpa's second wife. But, like scores of holidays, birthday parties, and funerals, we came together as one big family. It was Grandpa's way–the only way any of us knew.

We ventured in the small house and there sat Grandpa on the brown couch surrounded by his daughters. When we appeared through the throng of people, his bright blue eyes sparkled.

As the day wound down and people began to leave, the vibe of the room changed. I was the last of our foursome to say goodbye and I was not going to rush it–this was an important moment for us both, perhaps our last goodbye.

I took his tiny face in both of my hands, not caring what anyone would think.

The crowded room became perfectly still.

I whispered in his ear, "I love this guy," then pulled his face back so that we were nose to nose.

Our whiskered cheeks scraped together and I whispered the words a second time.

"I *love* this guy."

For that moment, it was just the two of us in the world. With our eyes locked, Grandpa gave a quick nod. No other words were necessary.

I blinked and looked around the room. Every face of every daughter, granddaughter, and daughter-in-law beamed with a look of pure love. Everyone was crying in silence. The men in the room avoided eye contact. I smiled at everyone and turned to leave. At the front door I turned back and looked him in the eyes one last time. He smiled and nodded. That was last time I saw him.

• • •

That's not actually a true statement.

Exactly one week later, I awoke from a dream in the early Sunday morning hours. The room was dark but light filtered in from the sliding glass door in the corner of the room.

I blinked and *it shone next to me on my left.*

I shook my head to clear the cobwebs of sleep and my eyes began to adjust to the light filtering in from the streetlamp outside.

It sparkled and shimmered.
Formless and floating.

I blinked again, convinced that I *was* awake and whatever was hovering next to me was what caused me to open my eyes.

As my pupils began to focus in the dark, it raced to the foot of the bed.

I held up my hand to say *Don't Go* but before I could get the words out, it flew through the curtained sliding glass doors and was gone.

After years of playing these seconds in my mind, the best description I can give is that it was *pure energy*; sparkly and free-floating.

The phone rang about 9 a.m. Mom was on the line.

"They just called," she said. "Your grandpa passed away early this morning. I'm so sorry, baby."

I smiled.

"I know. He came by on his way out."

Then I told her what happened.

> Garden Hose Lesson Learned:
> Love is stronger than blood
> if you're lucky enough to discover it.

1 2

Damon Wayans is right

From time to time I meet up with my good friend and former college confidante, Joe. He lives in Bakersfield and I live in Seattle, so the logical place to catch up is Las Vegas.

Well, logical to us anyway.

We've had ourselves some adventures there during the college daze–uh, *days*.

In the year 2000 I scored us tickets to see Damon Wayans at the Hilton. Anyone who's a product of the eighties surely remembers Damon's characters and epic one-liners:

"Banana Man" in *Beverly Hills Cop* ("Here brother, take these bananas."),

"Willie" in *The Hollywood Shuffle* ("Just follow the trail of empty activator bottles to Jerry Curl's crib, Mr. Ace."), and

"T-Bone" in *Colors* ("We gonna put the bite on Pac-Man's ass. Now go get me some cigarettes and a dirty magazine!").

If not, perhaps Damon is best known for stealing most every scene during the four year run of *In Living Color* in the early nineties.

Yeah, we adore Damon, no two ways about it.

Joe and I settled into our high-backed booth and I couldn't help but marvel that this was the *same theater* where Elvis thrilled the previous generation. Elvis hasn't left *this* building as you have to walk past a life-size bronze statue of him in the lobby. (I have a picture of Mom holding the bronze hand—one of those "Ahhh" moments for me. Hey, the next time you're in the Vegas Hilton take a hold of the bronze hand and think of me.) In my mind I pictured the night in 1974 when Mom traded three long stem red roses for a white scarf and sweaty kiss from the King of Rock 'N Roll. She saw the King seven times over the years, all from the vantage point of a front-row booth. When she went to see Elvis with her brother Harold, they went *in style* and that scarf became her most prized possession—the single line-item in her simple will: *The scarf will go to Hannah*.

A magical place, the ballroom of The International. Oops, I mean the Las Vegas Hilton.

Twenty six years after Mom's experience with Elvis, Damon strolled out to thundering applause. His bald head shone as if he'd just had it waxed. The guy personified *cool*. With the confidence and poise of a man who's got his, uh, *act* together, he launched into his routine.

Two jokes have stayed with me and the first went something like this:

"It's a sad testament these days when a medication's side effects are worse than the condition it's supposed to treat. One medicine to treat indigestion causes *greasy* discharge. (He pronounced it GREE-ZEE.) Now I don't know what's worse but I think I'd prefer to avoid *gree-zee* discharge at all costs."

Damon laughed at his own joke and the capacity crowd laughed with him. He paced around the empty stage thoroughly enjoying himself, occasionally drinking water from a glass on a solitary bar stool.

"I just turned forty. Forty changes a man. I took my girls to dinner the other night and excused myself to the restroom . . .

So I'm taking a pee.

(He strikes the pose for maximum visual effect.)

I shake it . . .

Zip up . . .

Then pee *summore*."

When the riotous laughter finally subsided, Damon concluded, "It's a bitch getting old."

Let's see.

Degrading vision?

Check.

Male pattern baldness (but desperately waiting for the Rogaine foam to kick in)?

Check.

Gotta get up and pee at 2 a.m. *every damn night?*

Check.

Damon's right.

It *is* a bitch getting old!

[Note: For the better part of a year, I was convinced that the title of this book would be: "Damon Wayans Was Right and Other Lessons I've Learned Along the Way."

I like that title but realized that my odds of getting in touch with Damon and getting permission to use his name and likeness was about as good as being the first successful prostate transplant candidate.

So, I went the Garden Hose route which doesn't, in any way, diminish how cool Damon Wayans is to me.]

> Garden Hose Lesson Learned:
> Eventually your hose is gonna leak!

1 3

JC, my favorite DJ

Unfamiliar with the *miracle of birth* since I'm not a father and chose to take a pass on watching Chloe enter this world (I love my sister-in-law to pieces but she scared me to death when she asked if I'd be in the room to which I gently said, "Uh, thank you but *nooooo*."), my miracles seem to manifest themselves when I need them the most.

You may call them coincidences. I call them God's intervention in this tiny, insignificant life of mine. You'll read about more than one during your time with me in this book. Here's the first:

While Susan and I strolled through the 2006 Seattle Home Show, my brother, David, found himself *one with the backboard*–completely immobilized–staring up at the bright lights of the Emergency Room in Roseville,

California. The neurosurgeon's face emerged in his limited field of vision.

"Do you have *any* feeling below your mid-chest?"

David answered, "Of course. Why wouldn't I?"

The doctor's eyebrows raised.

"Because I have never seen this injury without permanent paralysis."

David closed his eyes but couldn't stop the hot tears streaming into his ears.

• • •

I had just left him a voicemail–

"Keep it on two wheels, Slick. Nobody's gonna care what place you took tomorrow."

–knowing he was racing the amateur Arenacross at Arco Arena in Sacramento. Arenacross is the Reader's Digest version of Supercross where professional motorcycle racers, most young and fearless, fly over 80-foot triple-jumps thrilling thousands of cheering spectators in sold-out football stadiums across the country.

David seems to have taken most of the competitive instinct between the three Harvey bros–and it probably doesn't help that we grew up loving Burt Reynolds in the 1978 stuntman movie, *Hooper*. As I've told him more than once, "Brother, you are Sonny Hooper to me. Porn 'stauche and all!"

As Knucklehead pinned the throttle to pass the guy that had just passed him–because second place is *not cool, not cool at all* and it *was* the last lap (and never mind little brother's sage advice)–it happened in an instant.

[Insert the Shangri-Las 1964 hit song, *Leader of the Pack* here:

Look out! Look out! Look out! Look out! Keee-rash! SPLAT!

If there's one thing our stepdad did right, besides fathering my little sister, it was letting us listen to his Shangri-Las reel-to-reel in the mid-70s.]

David flew over the bars and drove himself head-first into the rock hard dirt. Dazed, confused, and with a burning sensation in his back, he thought he'd catch his breath, stand up and push his bike back to the truck. That's *one way* to finish a night of racing and there *is* an embarrassment factor involved with crashing–something I know quite a lot about. Perennial friend, Lance Beauchamp–it's pronounced BEE-CHUM; but I pronounce it SUPER-MAN–ran over and kept David horizontal while the medics scrambled over. Of course stuntmen and professional (correction: *amateur*) motocross racers are super tough, so David was ready to stand up and remove himself from the spotlight.

"Nah," Lance said, "let's see what the medics say."

• • •

The pit in my stomach told me that something wasn't right when "Tamara cell" flashed on my cell phone.

"Hey," I said tentatively.

"He crashed."

Inhale deep breath. Exhale loudly.

"How bad?"

"He's in the ambulance on the way to the hospital," my sister-in-law said, her voice wrought with tension. "Lance says he's immobilized and has back pain."

Back pain. Not good. Not good at all.

"Can he move his legs?"

"Yes."

"Oh, thank God."

We left the Home Show and Susan drove straight home. I curled up on the couch in the fetal position waiting for the phone to ring again.

"Hello?"

"Thomas, this is Lance."

"Lance. How's it going? What do you know?"

"He's being admitted. He can move his legs but . . ."

"BUT WHAT?"

"But, he had a CT scan and the doctor is pretty freaked out. He broke a vertebra off his spine. It's not good. He's going to need surgery."

"Great."

"One other thing," Lance said. "The doctor says there's no guarantee. The surgery may make things worse."

"What does that mean?"

"Means he's not paralyzed now. He could be afterward. I don't even want to think about what would have happened if he had tried to stand up after the crash."

I could barely breathe with invisible King Kong standing on my chest.

"Thanks for being there Lance. I'll see you soon."

Click.

"He needs spinal surgery," I whispered to Susan. "I need to be there."

"We'll go," she said, "this weekend while he's recovering."

"NO!" I shouted, my breath coming in quick gulps. "I need to be there! Before the surgery! I need to see him *before* the surgery! He may never walk again!" I was close to hysterics.

She hugged me, her eyes wide with surprise. "OK. OK. OK. Shhhhh."

My plan the next morning, a Monday, was to go into the office and make arrangements to be out for the rest of the week. With my head swimming, I climbed into my Toyota Tundra and turned the ignition key.

• • •

Dictionary.com defines *miracle* as "an event that is contrary to the established laws of nature and attributed to a supernatural cause; any amazing or wonderful event."

OK, I'm guilty of chuckling at other people's so-called miracles–the Virgin Mary's face in a Rice Krispie Treat–Jesus' face in a flour tortilla–so when it comes to apparitions and food, I suppose I'm a non-believer.

It was with a heavy heart that I sat in the truck trying to gather enough energy to make the 20-mile drive to work. The sound of the CD spinning up in the player was broken by these softly-spoken words:

> *There can be miracles*
> *When you believe*
> *Though hope is frail*
> *It's hard to kill*

This is the theme song of the 1998 animated movie, *The Prince of Egypt*.

Of the ten thousand songs in my iTunes collection, the odds of *When You Believe* playing at this exact moment are beyond my comprehension. As the truck idled in the cold morning frost, I began to cry.

But it wasn't tears of sorrow.

It was tears of *joy*.

I sat upright and concentrated on Mariah Carey and Whitney Houston's voices:

> *Who knows what miracles*
> *You can achieve*
> *When you believe*
> *Somehow you will*
> *You will*
> *When you believe*

I'm not going to go so far as to say–on second thought–yeah, *I am* going so far as to say that God commissioned Stephen Schwartz to write these lyrics–and Mariah and Whitney were born to sing the song–for *me*– for the *exact* moment I needed to hear these words.

This moment–*this divine intervention, this miracle*– took all of my fear away and I flew to Sacramento that day in a hell of a good mood. A miracle was coming. I knew it as fact.

Though my brother underwent a grueling surgery of titanium implants and bone transferred from his hip to his spine, *the guy can walk.*

The guy can run.

The guy can pick up his 3-year-old daughter.

The guy doesn't have any physical limitations as a result of his spinal injury.

Yes, God provides miracles.

God delivered on the promise because I *believed*. Thanks, JC, for spinning up that song when I needed it the most!

> Garden Hose Lesson Learned:
> JC can fix anything!
> You just gotta believe.

14

Choosing a doctor for your annual male exam. Yes, *that exam!*

A couple days back from the woods of North Carolina, I noticed the skin tag on the inside of my right thigh–about the size of a flax seed. Damon Wayans voice echoed in my mind, *It's a bitch getting old.*

I went to bed without a second thought.

A week passed and the skin tag grew.

It's a bitch getting old.

Another week passed and the thing was noticeably bigger so I gave it a tug.

It wiggled.

It freaking wiggled.

I grabbed the magnifying glass for a closer look. To my *utter horror*, I had been harboring a growing tick, comfortable as hell snuggled into my ball sack, for the last two weeks.

I ripped it out of my leg (knowing that probably wasn't the recommended course of treatment) and held it up to the light.

"How do you like *that*, you little bastard?" I swear to God I heard a tiny scream as I squeezed the life out of the repulsive insect.

I grabbed my doctor's business card out of my wallet and dialed the number.

"Dr. Fratelli's office. How can I help you?"

"This is Tom Harvey. I'm a patient there and I need to see the doctor right away. I just pulled a tick out of my leg!"

"One moment, please."

She covered the phone with her hand and said, "Uh, Dad? Tom Harvey's on the phone and he has a tick."

In a distant, muffled voice Dr. Fratelli said, "Who the hell is Tom Harvey?!"

He saw me that afternoon.

• • •

Dr. Fratelli is one cool cucumber.

In the healthcare world he's an anomaly. A guy who hangs his shingle as a solo practitioner employing his daughter to answer the phone and his wife to handle the bills. I'll be sad when he retires–this short, rotund 60-something Italian with bushy eyebrows, white hair, little stubby fingers, and a grin reminiscent of Joe Pesci.

He's double Board Certified in Internal Medicine and Oncology meaning that most of his patients are older than he is, many battling cancer.

Yeah, *It's a bitch getting old.*

I have to admit that, despite everything to the contrary, I actually enjoy going to the doctor. Well, *this* doctor anyway.

And prior to the big Four Oh, the only time I ever needed to see the man was for treatment of my bi-annual sinus infections. The visits were always the same once I was shown to the little exam room. Knowing what was in store, I'd take my long-sleeved dress shirt off and wait in my tank top.

Dr. F. would stroll in with my chart, his face lit with excitement.

"Tom, how are you?"

"You know, the usual sinus thing," I'd say thickly.

"Uh-huh."

He'd wrap both of his hands around my bicep and give a squeeze.

"*Nice* muscle definition! Let me listen to your chest."

Five minutes later I'd be out of there with a prescription and a fresh imprint of his stubby fingers all over my upper body.

All right, the guy's a groper.

No other way to really say it, but he gropes with the best intentions. That is to say, there's nothing sexual about his touch. He's simply a scientist who appreciates the wonder of the human body. I'm crazy about the guy so when we had *the talk*, I was ready to take our acquaintance to the 40-year-old guy level.

I'm talking about the annual male exam–also known as the *digital exam*–which almost makes it sound like you're getting your Timex serviced.

Back to the whole *It's a bitch getting old* thing, a guy can go half his life ignoring his prostate but, come forty, it's time to pay the piper. You would think that some smart guy somewhere would come up with a way to check the prostate with magic x-ray glasses. Hell, I'd pay full-billed charges for *that* exam, but that's not reality, friends.

So *Happy Birthday To Me* and all of that. Like a good healthcare consumer, I made an appointment for my first digital exam in 2008. The meet up with Dr. F. was two weeks out and, to be honest, I sweat bullets as the days got closer. Like a goof, the dumbest questions in the known universe flashed through my pathetic brain:

Is he gonna chuckle and say, "Drop your pants and grab your ankles?"

Are we gonna exchange uncomfortable small talk and share a cigarette afterward?

WTH does the prostate even do?

The fateful day arrived and I took my seat between two old wheezing guys in the small waiting room.

Fifteen minutes passed.

Sweat started to saturate my shirt even though the room was pleasantly air-conditioned.

The jolly old nurse appeared in the door with an exuberant, "Yooooooou're next!"

Great.

So I'm sitting on the exam table wondering how being violated for the first time in my life is going to play out and cursing God for inventing the walnut-sized organ-of-uselessness placed oh-so-disadvantageously in the male body.

Dr. F walks in and chuckles.

Damn. He's chuckling. He's gonna say, "Drop your pants..."

"You know, I'm really not looking forward to this," I said, staring at my shiny black penny loafers.

"And you think I am?!"

With that, he proceeded in the most clinical of ways. Nah, I won't go into detail other than to say I survived.

It wasn't *that* bad.

With the lube, that is.

See you next year, Doc.

Garden Hose Lesson Learned:
Fellas, at some point you're going to have to bend over and grab your ankles.
Try to make the most of it.

15

You will stand on your mother's grave

The hospice nurse walked out of Mom's small bedroom and quietly closed the door behind her.

"I know your mom," she said in the present tense.

Nice touch.

"She was a nurse at Roseville Convalescent Hospital, right?"

"Yes, she was."

"I've seen her there many times. I'm sorry, but . . . she doesn't have a heartbeat."

Not, *She's dead . . .* or, *She expired . . .* or, *She's not breathing*.

NO, REALLY? TELL ME SOMETHING I DON'T KNOW!

I didn't say anything but forced a smile.

"Do you want me to wait with your family for the Chapel of the Roses guy?"

"Do you usually?"

"Well . . . not usually, no."

"No thank you then. Go home and be with your family."

It was, after all, Thanksgiving.

When the non-descript, windowless white van pulled into the driveway an hour later, waves of nausea rolled up from my stomach. As the guy unloaded the gurney, soon to fill the body bag with the lifeless form that was my mother, I walked out into the street and the cold night air.

Forty minutes passed.

Shaking from the cold and light-headed from the unimaginable, surreal situation, I thought, *What is taking so long?*

When I teetered back in the house, the now-occupied gurney stood just inside the front door. The zipper rested at Mom's chin. The rest of her small body was covered by a heavy, bright-blue blanket.

"Do you want to be the one to cover her face?" David asked.

I shook my head, *No*.

David gently covered her face with the blanket and the little guy from the funeral home wheeled Mom out the door and toward the driveway. When he collapsed the legs of the gurney and slid it into the empty hold of the van, one voice in my brain whispered, *Her head is near the tail pipe. She shouldn't have gone in feet first.*

Another voice whispered, *Does it really matter?*

"Hey," I called, "do you know any Elvis tunes?"

"Sure."

Tears cascaded down my face in long, burning streaks.

"Can you sing a couple on the way?"

"I'm not much of a singer but I'll hum a few. How's that?"

"I think that works."

The van pulled away, the contents headed for a refrigeration unit kept at a constant forty degrees.

• • •

Death is a part of life. It's a cliché but it's the truth.

As Robin Williams said in *Dead Poets Society*:

We are food for worms, lads. Each and every one of us in this room is, one day, going to stop breathing, turn cold, and die.

A few weeks earlier, my mother spoke the saddest words I've ever heard.

My sister, Tricia, holding vigil at her bedside said, "We're losing you, Mom. What are we going to do without you?

Mom whispered, "I'm losing *all* of you. What am *I* going to do?"

We've never been an overly religious family but with death close at hand, I wished my mother would have made peace with God. In the last hours of her life, I prayed over her; my lips pressed against her cool forehead; my hand stroking her dark hair. I prayed that the Lord Jesus Christ would forgive her sins; prayed that He would accept her into the kingdom of Heaven.

I look back at the end of 2008 with gratitude and humility. We had her for 49 days after the cancer diagnosis. In those irreplaceable days, I asked *her* to forgive *me* for all the lame things I put her through.

"I am so sorry, Mom. I am so, so sorry. Where do I even begin?"

As the tears soaked her shoulder, she whispered, "There's nothing to be sorry about baby."

These simple words lifted the weight of the world off my shoulders.

I cling to these words every single day.

• • •

Twenty years earlier, I had a co-worker named William at Sierra View District Hospital. A retired Army chaplain in his 70s, he was the hospital's go-to-Jesus-guy with not a lot to do. We shared countless hours in his office talking about college, women, and college women.

"Tell me something very wise," I said one day. "Something that took you many, many years to learn. *Enlighten me.*"

Behind him was a large poster of the cosmos with an arrow pointing to a tiny speck. The caption read: You are here.

Will leaned forward and his booming voice fell to a whisper.

"One day you will stand on your mother's grave . . ."

He inhaled through his nose and slowly exhaled through his mouth. His clear blue eyes became distant.

". . . and wish that you had told her you loved her, just . . . one . . . more . . . time."

We were nose to nose but he was looking right through me.

He blinked and leaned back in his chair. A smile crossed his face but his eyes were flooded with tears.

"Huh. Got anything a little less heavy? My mom's only 43 and she's got a long life still ahead of her."

He thought for a moment and blew his nose loudly in a white cotton handkerchief that seemingly appeared out of midair.

"Yeah. You know you're old when you sit down on the toilet and your balls hit the water."

The words of my wise friend William, long since gone himself, play in my mind every time I stand at her headstone. Through the tears, I whisper, *I love you Mother*, but I know she's not there. As sad as the lonely cemetery is, I can't help but think about ball splashing and chuckle.

Mom would laugh, too.

> Garden Hose Lesson Learned:
> Death and humor are a part of life.
> They can co-exist if you let them.

1 6

Goodbye Gunkles

[Note: This is the longest chapter in the book. After reading it, I hope you'll forgive me for the winding path this story weaves.]

Harold's first cousin, Theresa, and I looked at each other as the doctor walked in, squeezed one of Harold's toes, and said quietly, "We're within twenty minutes now."

It was 2:00 p.m. on Wednesday, June 10, 2009, and we were the only people in the room at the hospice facility in Simpsonville, South Carolina. Theresa, God bless her, had spent the night in a chair next to the bed and hadn't slept at all. Elvis' "2nd To None" CD played softly in the background.

I sent out the text: 20 minutes.

Theresa and I watched Mom's beloved older brother in silence–the rhythmic rise of the sheet covering his cancer-ravaged body almost indiscernible now.

No way he's going to die with Elvis playing. No way. He's waiting for the CD to end, I just know it.

Theresa stepped out of the room with ten minutes left on the doctor's prediction and my uncle did something he hadn't done in over a week. His lips quivered. His fingers twitched. In my mind, I told myself that in this last private moment he wanted to say something to me–his final goodbye. But he hadn't had any food or drink–unconscious for the last ten days–and simply didn't have the strength to utter a single word.

I whispered, "I know Uncle. I know. I'm so proud of you. It's OK. Go to your family. Mom's waiting for you. Go to her."

The room had suddenly gone quiet, the last song on the Elvis double CD (*Rubberneckin*) had finished.

Theresa reentered the room. The nurse followed behind her and asked softly, "How's it go---?"

I held up my hand.

"I think that was his last breath."

"I'll get the doctor," the nurse whispered.

Theresa and I looked at each other, hardly able to breathe.

The doctor must have been just outside the door because he appeared within seconds. He checked Harold's pulse and said, "I'm sorry, but he's gone."

I burst into tears and groped for the sliding glass door that lead to the outside patio. No one went after me, and I'm thankful for that.

I sent another text: *Uncle Harold left us at 2:24 p.m. God bless him.*

My niece Hannah, whom Harold lovingly nicknamed *Pooka Pooka*, was the first to respond: *Gunkles was a good man. He will be missed.*

The nurse taped paper angel wings to the door–signifying that Harold had done what he was there to do–and Theresa and I walked out arm-in-arm to the parking lot. I climbed into Harold's Dodge van and threw the Elvis CD on the passenger seat.

I looked down at Elvis' smiling face and smiled back.

• • •

My first memory of him was the time he appeared and Mom disappeared. *For a week!* And you know what? It's traumatic for a 6-year-old to be without his mother for more than fifteen minutes, so I honestly can't say I loved Uncle Harold in 1974. It didn't matter to me that they were going to see Elvis, front row, at The International in Las Vegas. I wanted my mom back, *immediately if not sooner!*

You could say my Uncle Harold was Elvis' biggest fan and he had the means: as a desk clerk/baggage handler for Eastern Airlines, he crisscrossed the country, *on Eastern's dime*, following his idol from show to show.

Saw Elvis more than 250 times.

Took more than 5,000 concert photos.

Bootlegged dozens of shows on his bulky cassette recorder.

By today's definition, you may regard him as a fan of Stalker Proportions. But Harold simply loved the King.

The King, in turn, knew Harold by name and acknowledged him in the front row of hundreds of shows.

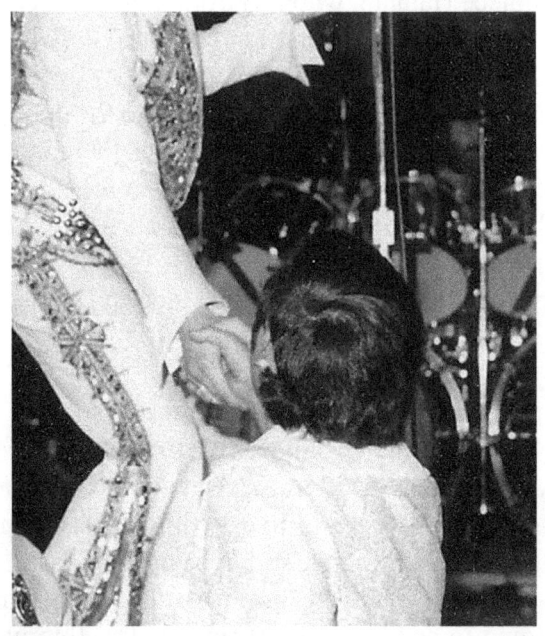

Harold shaking hands with a real famous guy.

• • •

We got Mom's death sentence ("cancer all over the place") in September, 2008 and I immediately called the longtime, elusive bachelor in South Carolina.

"We need you here, Harold."

"I don't know, Son," he said in his heavy southern accent. "I came out when your grandma was sick in '94 and ended up staying nine months. She wouldn't let me leave. Besides, all your mom needs is *a spark*. She needs to find *a purpose*."

"Mom is dying!" I shouted through the tears. "If you don't come out now, you won't see her again! I want you here. *For her!*"

Little did we know that, at the time, he was also dying of cancer.

After an hour of negotiating–and pleading, shouting, and crying on my part–he finally agreed. God bless him, he stayed for the duration and I spent the next ten weekends flying between Seattle and Sacramento watching the rapid decline of my precious mother's health.

One weekend near the end, I brought the *Elvis: That's The Way It Is* DVD and sat back to watch his reaction. Harold, on the edge of the sofa–his eyes brighter than I had ever seen before–grabbed my arm repeatedly and said things like, "Look at the magic! Pure energy! The best ever! There'll never be another!" I had transported Harold back to an earlier era and, for that hour, I was more than just one of his five nephews. I was a confidante. I was a friend.

Wow, Harold loved Elvis Presley.

Literally loved the guy.

• • •

Mom died on Thanksgiving night, 2008 and, come Saturday, Harold was on a flight back to Greenville.

"You're not staying for the funeral?" I asked.

"Nah, Son," he said. "I don't like funerals."

Who was I to argue with *that?*

• • •

After nearly five years on the job, I was laid off on Friday, May 29, 2009.

It happens.

On Friday, May 29, 2009, my sister, Tricia, called.

"Harold's in the hospital. They think he had a stroke last night. Can you go back there and assess the situation?"

Can I go back to Greenville, South Carolina to "assess the situation?"

"Well, I guess so, but I've got a first-class Amtrak ticket to Raleigh on June 2, so *I can only stay a few days.*" With the severance package and the reality that there are only so many times in a guy's life he can leisurely meander across the country, I was going to take full advantage of my temporary unemployed status.

Eight hours after that phone call I was on a plane to Greenville via San Diego and Atlanta. I was supposed to arrive Saturday night and meet up with second cousins I had never met before.

Saturday morning, nestled comfortably in my first class seat, the plane began its descent into San Diego–and then it changed course and threw me back in the seat.

"Fog's too thick in San Diego so we're diverting . . ." the pilot announced.

Awesome. My connecting flight window was only an hour.

". . . to Palm Springs."

When the fog eventually broke, I arrived in San Diego three hours late and had to wait for the redeye to Atlanta eight hours after that. After a sleepless night on the plane, I had a sleepless four hour layover waiting for the commuter plane to Greenville. I finally arrived in Greenville, South Carolina nearly a full day behind schedule.

I called my second cousin, Theresa, with the news that I was going straight to the Comfort Inn since I was in desperate need of comfort–and seeing double vision from exhaustion.

These lost hours, twenty two in all, changed everything.

After four hours of the deepest sleep I've ever known, I dragged myself out of the dark, comfortable room and drove the rental car to the hospital. Thank you Garmin GPS.

I took a deep breath and hit speed-dial to the second cousin I had never met before.

"I'm here."

"We're in the ICU on the fifth floor. We'll be right down."

Now I wouldn't have known Theresa from the Virgin Mary so when the smiling, weary couple walked straight up to me for the group hug, I seriously hoped they had the right guy.

"Theresa?"

"Tom?" she asked in her southern drawl.

We sat down in the lobby and Theresa and her husband, Lewis, looked at me expectantly.

"I'm no lawyer," I said, "but I printed out Power of Attorney documents here. Do you want Power of Attorney or do you want me to have it?"

Neither of us wanted it.

There! I said it.

"We'd like *you* to have it," Lewis said.

Theresa nodded.

I smiled.

Hell, why not? Sure, I'll take it! Whatever "it" was I had no idea.

We rode up the elevator to the 5th floor and walked into the brightly-lit, noisy Intensive Care Unit. With a central nursing station in the middle of the room, the only thing separating the seriously jacked-up patients in the ICU were curtains.

As I approached Harold, the words of my sister echoed in my mind:

Call him Gunkles. He likes that.

Fighting back tears, I took a deep breath and said, "Hi Gunkles."

Through an oxygen mask strapped over his nose and mouth, his face lit up.

"T-Man! The man with the plan!"

"We were just watching NASCAR," Lewis said. "Who won the race, Harold?"

Harold, propped up 45 degrees with a small TV on a retractable arm, spoke the last word he'd speak in this life: "Jimmie!"

[For those of you interested in which race occurred on Sunday, May 31, 2009, I'll spare you looking it up. It was the Autism Speaks 400 at Dover International Speedway.]

I'm just glad that Dick Trickle wasn't in the race and won it–for obvious reasons.

I pulled up what can best be described as a barstool on wheels and took his hand. He looked at me through loving eyes. He knew that I was *on the job*, nearly 3,000 miles from home. I was the man. *The man with the plan.*

Harold closed his eyes and began snoring. I squeezed his hand in short, firm clenches.

"They have him on some pretty serious medication," Lewis said.

I nodded.

"Well, we're going to take off now," Theresa said. They lived 75 miles away in Bessemer City, North Carolina and hadn't slept in nearly two days. "We'll check in with you tomorrow."

"OK."

And just like that, I found myself sitting in a hospital, surrounded by the swirl of activity and noise that critical patients require, with the most alone feeling I'd ever felt in my life.

We'll have to talk about this Power of Attorney thing tomorrow.

It was soon apparent that family members did not stay the night in the ICU, unless I knew how to sleep upright on a round chair with wheels surrounded by blinding lights and buzzing machines.

After giving the nurse my name and cell phone number (though Theresa had already informed everyone that "the nephew was on his way from Seattle and would be making all the decisions"), I drove back to the hotel and fell asleep as soon as I flopped on the bed.

When morning arrived I called the hospital. The shift change was in process but the nightshift nurse took my call.

"Mr. Harvey?"

"Yes."

"You're the nephew from Seattle?"

"Yes."

"Your uncle had a seizure last night."

"What does that mean, exactly?"

"It means you need to talk to the doctor."

"I'll be right there."

What else did I have to do? I was unemployed and 3,000 miles from home.

When I entered the ICU for the 2nd time, Harold was still snoring loudly. I sat on the barstool without drawing the attention of anyone. Eventually a gal strolled in and introduced herself as the social worker.

"So," she asked, "have you come to any decisions?"

"Decisions? Decisions about what?"

"Haven't you talked to the doctor?" she asked with panic in her voice.

"I've talked to one nurse since I've been here. Other than that, I don't know a *damn* thing."

She groped for her cell phone, hit speed dial and scurried down the hall. I began walking toward her but she held up a finger. *Stay.* Then she turned her back to me.

"Nephew here . . . doesn't know . . . need to speak with you *now* about Mr. Newton!"

The fact that she was berating a doctor would have been comical had I not felt that she knew something–something bad–that I didn't. She flipped her phone closed and said, "Come on. We're going to meet with your uncle's doctor."

• • •

She left me in a room the size of a bathroom stall and I stared at the wall in silence for twenty minutes. I had just nodded off when the door swung open and a chubby black guy in a white jacket stepped in and sat down in the only other chair in the small room. When he opened his mouth to speak, I noticed that half of his teeth were missing.

This guy's a doctor? What the f---?!

"I'm Dr. Greenbaum. I've been assigned to your uncle."

"I work in healthcare. What's your specialty?"

"I'm an Internist with specialized training in Palliative Care."

"I'm familiar with what you do. Thanks for taking care of him."

"You're welcome. Your uncle's a *very* sick man. Do you know the extent of his condition?"

"Like I told the social worker, I just got here from Seattle last night and I've talked to one nurse. All I know is that he apparently had a stroke two nights ago, he had a seizure last night, and now he's snoring like hell in the ICU."

I smiled.

The doctor smiled back.

I immediately liked the guy. OK, so doctors can have bad teeth like anybody else.

"There's no easy way to say this so I'll just say it. Your uncle didn't have a stroke. We did a brain scan and . . . he has nineteen metastasized brain lesions."

From here his pace quickened.

"You may get a visit from the radiation oncologist who wants to radiate him but I'm not in favor of that course of action."

Lightheaded, I nodded.

"In fact, he may not even survive the transfer from the ICU to the linear accelerator. Um, your uncle that is, not the oncologist."

I nodded again. The room started to spin. *Information overload!*

"Even though the machinery is on this campus, it's a bit of a hike," he continued.

"Will I be able to talk with him? My uncle, that is. I have quite a lot of questions."

He smiled a mostly toothless smile but with sad eyes said, "He's on very strong anti-seizure medication now. I don't think he'll regain consciousness again. Had you arrived a day sooner."

I closed my eyes to squelch the tears. A day earlier I was sitting in San Diego waiting for the midnight flight to Atlanta.

"Well, I'm not going to have him radiated, that's for damn sure." After saying the words, I paused. *I am making a life and death decision here. Oh my God.*

"I'm glad to hear that. I want to transfer him to my care on the Palliative Care floor. Are you in favor of that?"

"Yes."

"Oh. Apparently he's been receiving treatment at the veteran's hospital in Atlanta so we've requested a copy of those records."

"He has nineteen brain tumors. What do those records matter now?"

The doctor smiled again.

"Well, you got me there, Mr. Harvey."

• • •

As the social worker and I walked back to the ICU, I broke the silence.

"You know what I find interesting?"

"What, Mr. Harvey?"

"Here I am making life and death decisions for one of your patients and no one has even bothered to ask for identification. Not that it would do any good since my last name isn't the same as the patient's anyway. Hell, I could be some psycho mental freak that goes from hospital to hospital acting like God!"

She stopped in her tracks, her eyes widening.

"Oh, well . . ." she stammered, "I'm sure we'll be doing a background check on you . . . or something."

"I'm sure you won't," I smiled. "I just find this whole thing surreal, that's all."

• • •

The little two-bedroom house Harold rented off the beaten path was a mess. I got a key from the next-door neighbor who happened to be the landlord.

Elvis was everywhere. Framed pictures. Hundreds of albums. CDs. Old collectable TV Guides.

Ashtrays overflowed with cigarette butts.

Stacks of shirts and slacks hung on the back of the couch.

Dozens of empty Lucky Strike cigarette packs (which I threw away before learning that Harold was saving up for a nylon jacket, *dang*) were piled two feet high next to the small kitchen table.

Loose change was stacked on every available inch of dust-covered bookshelf.

The place reeked of stale cigarette smoke.

I dialed David's cell.

"I'm standing in Harold's house. There's pizza still in the box on the couch. Cans of franks and beans, the really cheap stuff, in grocery bags on the floor in the kitchen."

When I saw the cold green beans in the pot on the stove, I burst into tears.

I don't remember what my brother said to console me but the reality that my uncle would never come back to any of this–his house, his life, his *world*–hurt like nothing I'd ever known.

Mindlessly I began filling an empty gallon water jug with dusty nickels, dimes, and quarters. What else was there to do?

Over the next several days, I went between the hotel, the hospital, and Harold's house. The guy didn't throw *anything* away or so it seemed, and there *had* to be some instructions for what he wanted done in this FUBAR of a situation.

I cancelled my cross country Amtrak trip.

• • •

"What is he still doing here?" the doctor demanded.

This wasn't Dr. Greenbaum but one of his associates. Going on the sixth day of unconsciousness, Harold was better suited for a lower level of care and this doctor wasn't at all shy about sharing his opinion.

"If you think you're going to transfer him to a SNF, you've got another thing coming! My mom worked in a SNF and it was a terrible place."

[SNF stands for Skilled Nursing Facility and my mom was constantly working double shifts because staff just didn't come to work. Sorry to generalize here but I was not about to let Harold die in one of them. And to be perfectly fair, there could have been a wonderful 5-star SNF in the area but I wasn't interested in taking on the challenge of finding it.]

"Mr. Newton is tying up valuable resources!"

"By the looks of it, you're not full on this floor so you've got the room! If you're concerned about your Medicare statistics just say so!"

The doctor's mouth gaped open but he couldn't find the words.

"I'll talk to Dr. Greenbaum about this, but not you. So why don't you just take a hike!"

With the loudest "*HMPF!*" he could muster, the doctor disappeared out of the doorway.

Twenty minutes later, Dr. Greenbaum appeared–his toothless grin a mile wide.

"Heard you had a little chat with my associate, huh?"

We walked into the hallway.

"Yes, I did. What a dick. I'm definitely off his Christmas card list."

Dr. Greenbaum smiled again.

"I can see you're well educated on the healthcare delivery system so let me be clear with you. Your uncle's stay at this point reflects negatively on my Medicare statistics. This is my floor. My baby. Medicare would prefer a lower cost for the services your uncle is now receiving. You know that, right?"

"Yeah."

"And you know that we're not doing anything for him medically so he can be treated at a much lower level of care?"

"Yeah."

I looked in at the tray of untouched, cold scrambled eggs and over-buttered toast. Pangs of guilt rolled through me as it became clear I was causing this compassionate doctor grief.

"That said, Tom . . ." (we were long past Mr. Harvey) ". . . I'll keep him here to the end if that's what you want."

"He will *not* die in a SNF!" I swiped a tear streaking down my cheek.

"I didn't say anything about a SNF. There happens to be an inpatient hospice facility fifteen miles from here. Would you consider that?"

"I don't know. If I gave the ICU a 2 and your Palliative Floor an 8, on a scale of 1 to 10, how would the hospice facility rate?"

"Twenty!"

• • •

Two miracles appeared later that day as I made an appointment to tour the hospice facility in nearby Simpsonville, South Carolina.

In my sleep-deprived state, I didn't notice that the facility was located via *toll* road–and my old Garmin with its outdated maps didn't bother to mention it. As the miles rolled past, I noticed with increasing trepidation that the exit tollbooths weren't manned. You either had the fifty cents to throw in the basket or a camera took a picture of the violation for a ticket in the mail. Looking around in panic, I knew I didn't have any coins.

But there it was on the floorboard.

The gallon jug full of Harold's change. ($118 worth when I eventually cashed it in!) Why I had mindlessly scooped up all the change and put it in the van a few days earlier–well, I guess there was a reason after all.

Despite the fact that behind every door lay a dying person, the 30-bed Open Arms Hospice facility looked like a 5-star hotel: bright, clean carpets; tasteful art on the walls; plenty of windows that looked out on the surrounding lush acreage. Cheerful nurses zipped up and down the hallways. There was a definite energy to the place and family members in the hallway noticeably possessed an air of optimistic satisfaction. For a place that should have reeked with the smell of death, the only smell I recall was from the pine trees swaying in the breeze. There was even a small lake just down the hill if a patient or family member wanted to go fishing! I was impressed–and dismayed–that the place was at full capacity. Not a single empty bed. By the time I left, Harold was #1 on the wait list, and I was left thinking, *So strange that I'm waiting for the next person in this place to die to make room for Harold to die.*

I drove back to the hospital with my stomach grumbling loudly. It was about 2 p.m. and, like most of the days during this time, I hadn't had a thing to eat until well past the lunch hour–in fact, some days I didn't eat at all. I had given blood the day before–I was eligible and needed to do something that felt important–so I was starving. With a Wendy's in the front parking lot of the hospital, I stopped in.

Dizzy from the shortage of blood, lack of food, and extreme humidity, I ordered a chicken sandwich and a salad and groped for the nearest table. My head spun as another long day in Greenville played out. I looked at my food, thought of the green beans back on Harold's stove, and the wave of emotion rolled up my throat. I was about to totally lose it and there was nothing I could do to stop it.

I took a deep breath to brace for the tears and my hearing *changed*. That's really the only way to describe it. The Muzak–the really crappy elevator kind–playing overhead in Wendy's was *familiar*. What was that tune? The tears held as my mind raced. *What was that tune?*

And then it hit me.

Of all the tunes in the entire world at all the times, it was *Somewhere In Time*–the theme song of Mom's favorite movie with Christopher Reeve. It was at the exact second–not a moment too early or late–as the emotion threatened to take over.

[I know this tune very well thanks to my brother, David, who saw Michael Crawford sing it in the Las Vegas show, *EFX*, that ran from 1995 to 2003. The ex-Phantom of the Opera sings a beautiful rendition of this, the theme song to the show.]

A single tear fell and I watched it drop into the salad as if from the third person.

The tune was all there was in the world and I was caught up in it.

I started laughing and crying at the same time.

Mom.
You're watching over me.
You're here.

Mom, I miss you so, so much.
I closed my eyes and cried into my napkin.
The music surrounded me; engulfed me. I was having an out of body experience.
The song ended and my acute hearing instantly faded.
It's going to all work out. I'm not alone after all.

• • •

Harold died on June 10, 2009 and I stayed another week looking for some cosmic direction on what to do with him and his belongings. About the time I was ready to give up on instructions of any kind, the receipt in his travel bag couldn't have been clearer.
Finally!
Torn, faded, and coming apart where it was folded, it was the original receipt from 1974 for the family burial plot my grandmother purchased at the New Tacoma Cemetery.
Harold wants to be buried next to his brother in Tacoma! Why else would he have this relic in his travel bag?
The revelation was exhilarating.
I flew home on June 17th with the plan to return for the month of July and vacate the overflowing house by July 31.

• • •

I spent nearly the entire month of July, 2009 at Harold's house as his ashes sat in a white box on the mantle–cremation was the only option after getting the

$25,000 quote to fly his body from Charlotte to Tacoma. What was it? Twenty five dollars a mile? I learned that the planes that fly in and out of Greenville are too small to accommodate a body in the cargo hold so I got a quote for the world's most expensive cab ride to the Charlotte airport. (OK, it wasn't a cab but, likely, another non-descript van with the AC at full blast. None of it mattered in the end since all I could afford was the $800 to have him reduced to a pile of ash by the local Neptune Society. My personal opinion is that he probably didn't prefer cremation but, you know, *dead guys can't be choosy!* Especially broke dead guys who don't leave any instructions for nephews to follow!)

After dozens of trips to the nearby dump, Goodwill and Post Office, the stacks began to resemble something that would fit in his van and a U-Haul trailer. The *long* road trip from Greenville to Seattle loomed ahead of me.

As the end of the month approached, I decided it was time to close his post office box. I had been there a dozen times mailing packages full of random Elvis memorabilia to Harold's many friends so the teenage kid behind the counter and I were familiar to each other.

"Hey, how would I go about closing a PO Box?" I asked.

"Which box?"

"Twelve seventy two."

"Twelve seventy two . . . twelve seventy two . . ." His mind searched for its owner. With wide eyes and panic in his voice, "Mr. Newton?! That's Mr. Newton's! Where's Mr. Newton?!"

His reaction surprised me and I felt a sudden pang in my chest. I turned slightly and felt the presence of five people in line behind me. How do I make *this* quick?

"Mr. Newton was my uncle. I'm sorry to say that he passed away last month and I've been mailing boxes of his stuff to his friends this whole time."

"Mr. Newton . . ." he whispered, his face a mixture of sadness and shock.

I smiled and looked at the floor.

"He was my favorite customer. Just the nicest man, Mr. Newton."

I nodded.

• • •

The rap on the screen broke the silence and when I opened the door, a blonde woman stood on the front steps.

"Hi," she said. "I don't mean to pry. And this may be totally inappropriate but . . ."

I tilted my head, puzzled.

". . . is this where Harold lives?"

"This was Harold's house, yes."

"Was? *What do you mean, was?*"

"I'm sorry. Who are you?"

Was she a bill collector? The answering machine was stacking up with increasingly agitated messages from the guy from Bank of America.

"Oh, I'm sorry. I'm the manager at The Cracker Barrel on Woodruff Road."

"Huh. Really?"

"My husband is an EMT and took a call to this address a few weeks ago. Well, he told me about the guy they took to the hospital and the patient sounded like Harold. We haven't seen him in weeks and all the girls are worried about him."

"Please, come in."

We sat on the couch. With the side door open and the box fan blowing out, the cigarette smell was fading fast.

"Harold was my uncle. I'm sorry but he passed away on June tenth. I'm packing all his things up and leaving for Seattle at the end of the month."

Her face began the Emotional Quiver and I quickly reached for some tissue.

"Oh, I was afraid of that," she said as she wiped the tears spilling from her eyes. "He was our favorite customer. Our absolute favorite."

"Please, tell me more."

"He came in three times a week and didn't even have to order. We were on top of his order before he even sat down. Booth 37. Always, booth 37. Grits, two eggs over easy, toast with no butter, and black coffee."

"Yeah, that's Harold all right."

We sat facing each other, our knees almost touching. She blew her nose.

"When was the last time you saw him?" I asked.

"He came in every Friday for late breakfast so it had to have been the last Friday in May. He acted *real* strange that day. Then my husband talked about the call they took at this address and it all sort of fit."

"Strange? How do you mean?"

"He was very off balance. Slurred his words like he had been drinking. All the girls thought it was very strange."

Swallowing back the rising emotion in my throat, I whispered, "He hadn't been drinking. He had nineteen brain tumors. You saw him hours before they overtook him."

"Oh that poor man! All the girls miss him *so much*. He was our favorite customer."

I chuckled and she looked at me, confused.

"I'm not laughing at you," I said, "but you should see the effect he had on the kid at the Post Office."

• • •

On July 31, I hit the road with the Dodge Caravan and U-Haul trailer crammed with Harold's life possessions. My first stop was Memphis, Tennessee and, with the help of Harold's friend and Elvis' former personal secretary, Becky Yancey, we had a Mission Impossible to do at Graceland.

[Becky has her own stories of the King; author of *My Life With Elvis*.]

After a long 525-mile drive through 5 states and a tornado, I found my way to Becky's house and happily occupied her spare bedroom. The following day we had VIP Graceland tour passes and *Operation Spread Some of Harold's Ashes at the King's Casa* was on.

Memphis in August is hot and humid, so I put on my cargo shorts (the kind with pockets down the thighs) and a Sun Records T-shirt. I carefully poured a cup of ash in a Ziploc bag prior to leaving Becky's house and away we went to Elvis Presley Boulevard. In a way, dumping remains (or *cremains*, if you prefer) at someone else's house is kind of gross. It's also illegal, I'm fairly certain, and would have definitely got us thrown off the property had we been caught. But, as Tom Cruise said in Risky Business, *Sometimes you gotta say WTF*. And that pretty much summed up the entire summer of 2009 for me.

As I pulled into the handicapped parking lot at Graceland (thanks to Becky's placard and emphysema from years of smoking), my left pocket began noticeably vibrating. I looked down and thought, *Must have my cell phone on vibrate*. My hand squished into the bag and, for a moment, I was dumbstruck. Then I started laughing.

"What's so funny?" Becky asked.

"It's Harold. He's excited to be here."

The phone was in my *right* pocket.

Harold, king of the comb-overs, in happier times–
and in whole-body form.

I know what you're thinking. That sounds like a cute, convenient way to end the story. Vibrating ashes my *ash!* But, that's how it happened. No more, no less. I swear it on Harold's *Grits, two eggs over easy, toast with no butter, and black coffee.*

Operation Ash Spread was a success. Thank you Becky!

Garden Hose Lesson Learned:
Listening to the King just might prolong your life!

17

If it were easy everyone would do it

It was my freshman year in high school, 1982-1983, when I discovered my *extreme* dislike for it. It was painful and wasn't any fun at all. Coach Q told us that once our bodies got used to it, we would enjoy it. I wasn't buying that line of crap and, really, the best part for me was the shower afterward.

Yeah, jogging just wasn't working for me.

The loop around the school, a large square about two miles long, was the longest hour of our lives. Coach thought he was clever throwing in competitive motivation but we just weren't into it.

[The entire class had a 1,000 yard head start on our star cross-country runner, Kevin Cardillo. While we pissed and moaned in the heat and *tried* to stay ahead of him, it was no use. Kevin would glide by effortlessly and we both admired and hated his guts for it.]

After my freshman year, I vowed never to run again. The whole exercise was futile.

That was 29 years ago.

• • •

I found myself mindlessly staring at the date: November 27, 2011.

My stomach hurt thinking about it and I was on the verge of tears–the three year anniversary of Mom's death.

The voice in my mind whispered, *Do something. Don't let it be a sad day. Do something special.* I turned away from the calendar pinned to my cubicle wall and clicked on the Seattle Times webpage.

And there it was.

An ad for the Amica Seattle Marathon.

But you don't like to run. In fact, you hate to run, the voice reminded me. *Remember the pain in your lungs? Remember that a**munch Kevin Cardillo? You hate to run. Forget it. Keep looking.*

"Now wait just a second," I whispered to myself. The previous two November 27th's were sad days and I was not about to make it three in a row.

A different voice chimed in.

You're gonna do it. It's only July so you have four months to prepare. You're gonna do the Seattle Marathon. It's decided.

And so that quickly, I had my cross to bear.

My dragon to slay.

My hero's quest.

I was going to run more than a hundred yards at a time. I was going to be a *runner*.

• • •

When I do something, I tend to go a little overboard and this crazy notion was no exception. Within days I had purchased four pairs of running shoes (all the *wrong* size–who would have known you need running shoes a half size bigger than your normal shoe?), bought an entire collection of outdated *Runner's World* magazines off eBay (overpaying the eager gal in the process but what the hell), bought a fancy schmancy Garmin GPS watch with heart rate monitor (yep, 180 beats a minute feels like death!) and bought way too many Dry Fit stretchy outfits. I had the equipment so *let the transformation begin!* And God bless my wife, Susan, for embracing this new activity. What a trooper!

The first thing I learned about running is that it's done in kilometers–as in the 5 and 10 varieties. And what sounds more impressive?

"I just ran 3.1 miles or *I just ran a 5k?*"

So let runners thumb their noses at the rest of us and use the *metric* system. They also use the word *fartlek* in everyday conversation. Look it up. I am not kidding.

I found this nasty little route from my front door that included this nasty big hill and away I went. It was just over four miles and after six tries, I could actually jog the whole thing without walking. *Victory!*

I busted through the door, out-of-breath, and drenched in sweat. "I didn't walk once! Are we ready for our first 5k?" Susan nodded enthusiastically.

From the bathroom I continued to study my outdated *Runner's World* stack in fifteen minute intervals (or until my legs fell asleep, whichever came first).

Don't start out too fast.
Don't line up in the front.
Hydrate but don't over-hydrate.
And don't, under any circumstance, throw elbows at the finish line in an attempt to claim victory over the 80-year-old dude or the lady pushing the stroller.

So much to remember!

The date was August 18, 2011 and the Foster Kids 5k just down the road at Marymoor Park was where I'd stick my toe in the water of my first competitive running event. By typical standards of which I am *now* familiar, the turnout was small, (about 100 casual weekend runners) but what did I know then? They all had numbered running bibs pinned to their shirts so this had to be a *race*.

I *would* be both demoralized and make a total ass of myself in the next 29 minutes and 18 seconds, but how could I have known it standing there at the starting line with Susan?

Bang!

The gun went off and the small group surged forward as one. I quickly left Susan behind as Twisted Sister sang, *We're not gonna take it! No, we ain't gonna take it!* in my headphones.

After the first couple hundred yards, I found myself impatient with two pre-teen girls painlessly having a conversation as they loped in front of me.

No elbows! Just ease on by! Hell, son, you're a runner!

Ozzy was belting out the live version of *Paranoid* as I extended my stride past these two inferior runners. Oh, this running thing is *so good* for the ego.

And then . . .

Out of the corner of my eye the gazelle caught my eye. In a flash, she passed by and quickly distanced herself.

You think you're sooooooooo cool, the demon whispered. *You just got passed by a pregnant woman pushing a double-wide stroller!*

My counter-voice objected, *That woman's gotta be 6' 2" and she's twenty years younger than you!*

The Truth Demon scoffed, *She's pregnant and pushing a stroller!*

Oh, I was pissed.

I made the turn at halfway and pushed forward, my lungs and legs burning but *pain is temporary! Glory lasts forever!*

That's right, dumbass, my demon giggled. *Burn yourself out! You're not gonna make the finish without walking!*

With a half mile to go and defiantly swallowing the pain shooting through my lungs, I spotted her. With the demon's pie hole suddenly shut, my voice of reason chimed in.

Your pace is faster. You can take her. Steady, man, steady!

I was gaining on her with every stride. This was possible.

She's yours! Take her, take her! Never mind that breather behind you, focus forward!

On my left, the ten-year-old loped past.

Don't worry about that kid! The girl! Focus on the girl! Here she comes now.

In the next instant, *a guy pushing a stroller* pulled up next to me and, seemingly, we were all racing to the bobbing blonde ponytail, now just 20 feet ahead of us with 100 yards to the finish.

Oh, hell no! Don't you get passed by a stroller! I don't care if it's Usain Bolt pushing it!

I opened my stride, pulling ahead of Stroller Guy and his wonky, loping ten-year-old. Ponytail Lady was on my right shoulder, her focus on the finish.

I looked over.

Ninety yards to go.

She looked straight ahead.

Eighty yards to go.

I looked over again.

Seventy yards to go.

She looked straight ahead.

I looked over *again.*

She finally looked over as Stroller Guy, Wonky Boy, and I pulled even on her left.

Her eyebrows narrowed, a look of confusion on her face.

"Well," I huffed, *"let's go!"*

She paused for another second before a smile spread across her face.

"OK."

We broke into a sprint. Stroller and Wonky disappeared from our peripheral vision.

Fifty, forty, thirty, twenty yards . . .

With ten yards to go my voice screamed, *Dumbass, noooooooooo! Don't throw elbows at the finish! Don't you dare beat her!*

In the last instant, I held up and she surged past at the finish stripe.

"Thanks!" she called out and turned back toward the finish line. Stroller Guy and Wonky Boy crossed the line and they celebrated together. Stroller Guy shot me a glare that said, *Go shove a red hot poker up your ass!*

I ducked behind a tree.

Nice going dipshit, my now vociferous demon laughed. *You blew the family finish! Whatta jackass!*

Susan crossed the line a few minutes later and I told her the gory details in the car.

• • •

By the time November 27, 2011 rolled around we had done half a dozen 5k's. With no shortage of optimism, I signed up for the *half* marathon (13.1 miles) reminding myself that *Mom would be proud! You don't have to run a full marathon.*

The cold, dark morning came quickly and Susan dropped me off at the base of the Space Needle. People threw elbows to use the two dozen Porta-Potties setup to handle *20,000 runners*–a scenario not specifically covered in *Runner's World*.

The gun went off and the running mob took off.

At the halfway point of the Half, I was in the zone: slugging it out, the rain dripping off my hat in large, cold beads–my pace at ten minutes a mile.

You've never run six and a half miles non-stop before! You're doing awesome, the encouraging voice whispered.

You're not done yet jackass! You are BARELY hanging on and the Madison Hill is coming, the *other* voice gloated.

Sadly, these voices *do* exist in my brain.

People cheered from both sides of the street as the dreaded Madison Hill came into view. I leaned forward, shortened my stride, and began to climb the slick, wet road.

The voices began arguing.

Don't walk! You can do it!

Walk! Walk! You can't do it!

My heart raced, my lungs burned, my legs ached. The voices kept screaming.

Don't walk! You can do it!

Give up sucker! Here comes two dozen Kevin Cardillo's now!

My heart rate was out of control and starbursts flashed in my vision. I couldn't get enough oxygen in my burning lungs. I had hit the wall at mile-marker 8. *Damnit!*

"OK, OK, we'll walk up the hill," I gasped.

Dozens of people–young, old, barefoot, pregnant– streamed around me.

It's fine! Really! We still have over five miles to go. No problem. But now that we've got that out of the way, get back to jogging on the downhill. It's freaking cold out here!

At mile-marker 11, my stride slowed to an eleven and a half minute pace and I was intermittently jogging and limping; both calves spasmed painfully.

My little angel voice chimed in, *Remember what you read in Runner's World? The last half mile will be euphoric. The cheering crowd will carry you along. You'll float to the finish line. Mom's watching from above.*

Really? the demon asked. *Why does every step hurt then?*

Too tired to run around potholes full of water, I splashed forward. Limp. Jog. Limp. Jog. Groan. Argh. Groan. Argh. People cheered and shouted encouragement from both sides of the street. My mind pictured the finish inside Memorial Stadium at the base of the Space Needle.

Where's the pain-free euphoria? the demon demanded. *This isn't pain-free! This hurts like hell! I'm cold! I'm hungry! I gotta pee! Hey, there's a Starbucks coming up on the left! Let's zip in for a nice little Fair Trade Certified Italian Roast! There's a bathroom in there too, Ace!*

"The finish line, the finish line, the finish line, the finish line," I mumbled.

"One more turn!" a course worker shouted. "You're almost there! You can do it!"

Entering the stadium with thousands of cheering spectators, the pain was replaced by newfound adrenalin and I sprinted past groups of weary runners.

"This is for you Mother," I croaked as my eyes flooded with tears.

"For you. For you. For you. For you."

I crossed the line at 2:21:51 and collapsed in a chair completely out of breath and blubbering in loud sobs. A worker draped a shiny foil blanket around me, distressed at my condition.

"Are you OK? Do you need a medic?" she screamed.

Not interested in sharing the moment with this well-intentioned stranger, I stood up and limped toward the exit corral. Tears blurred my vision. Snot streamed out of both nostrils. Brother, I was *spent!*

"Hey!" she shouted, "are you OK? Hey! *Hey!*"
I waved her off and began searching for Susan.

Limping away from the 2011 Seattle Half Marathon.

• • •

That was nearly two years and dozens of runs ago. While I can't say that I truly love running or am particularly good at it, I can say that we co-exist.

My victories are small–if I give it my all, I don't mind finishing slower than my personal record of 25 minutes, 11 seconds. When Kevin Cardillo zips by in the form of a ten-year-old kid or an 80-year-old lady, I'm OK with it.

Susan and I finished the Resolution Run 5k on New Year's Day, 2013 and we couldn't have been happier. Finishing at 29:05, it was far from my best but Susan summed it up like this:

"If it were easy, everyone would do it."

And I've *almost* reconciled with myself that the occasional baby stroller is going to blow by.

A baby stroller? OMG you suck!

Shut the hell up demon!

Garden Hose Lesson Learned:
Reinventing yourself is OK
if you can control the voices in your brain!

1 8

Musings

Leggo my Eggo!

If someone asked me if I loved Eggos when I was a kid, a simple *yes* was the answer. The frozen waffle that transformed into crispy-brown goodness with one click of the toaster was, in a word, *beautiful*.

If you ask a kid if he likes Eggos nowadays, the answer is not so simple.

Why? When's the last time you walked down the frozen-food aisle and looked for Eggos?

Would you believe that there are no less than twenty different flavors? At last count, there are actually twenty one. Wait! *Twenty two* thanks to Seasonal Pumpkin Spice. Blech! Seasonal Pumpkin Spice? I think I'll pass.

Twenty two different ways to *Leggo my Eggo!* Here are some of the more interesting ones:

- FiberPlus Antioxidants Chocolate Chip Waffles (say *that* three times fast).
- Nutri-Grain Low Fat Whole Wheat Waffles (I doubt that scores high on the ole Kid-o-Meter).
- My personal favorite, Simply Eggo Original Waffles.

Seriously, do we need all these varieties of Eggos?

But why stop at twenty two? How about Banana Daiquiri or Strawberry Margarita or Long Island Iced Tea-flavored Eggo?

No!

Bloody Mary-flavored Eggo for that ultimate Hair of the Dog That Bit Me morning after hangover. *Now* we're onto something.

Uh, it's a *hand* dryer . . .

Now that I'm on the downhill slide of physical fitness (at 45, the old muscle definition isn't what it used to be), I find myself at 24-Hour Fitness more and more. Let me tell you, *things have changed* since the college days.

Back in the day, people actually interacted with each other. If you found yourself staring up at two plates of bench-pressing machismo (translation: 225 pounds), you could pretty much expect to be staring up at a stranger's ball sack.

Which was comforting.

In other words, you could ask a guy to spot for you, thus avoiding finding yourself helplessly pinned under the heavy weight going for that elusive third rep.

Nowadays, it's every man for himself.

Everyone, including myself, is wired into their iPod personal universe.

No one makes eye contact.

Nowadays, it's just me and Muse's *Knights of Cydonia* to get me through the bench press. So it's *one* plate on either side (translation: 135 pounds) and more reps for this old cowboy. But I'm not complaining about *that*.

That's not to say I don't have a complaint for the old guy in the locker room who gives new meaning to the term *lift and separate*.

To you, Sir:

The hand dryer is just that–a machine that provides a whoosh of warm air to *dry your hands*. There's actually a little picture of hands being rubbed together for the illiterate. The thing is not a ball sack dryer! I *almost* admire the adaptability but, seriously Chief, use a freaking towel.

The *famous* Sonny Sanders

Adam "Sonny" Sanders was a famous country singer from Missouri living in the tiny Central California town of Terra Bella. In our small living room, Grandpa–*I mean, Sonny*–would plug his electric guitar in a small amplifier and perform for my brother and me. Front-couch seats for the famous entertainer!

Being the inquisitive ten-year-old, I worked up the nerve to ask the tough question.

"Grandpa, if you were so famous why can't we buy any of your records?"

His answer was always the same.

"Back in Missouri, (he pronounced it *MA-ZURA*) there was a gal who bought every one she could find."

"She bought *all of them?*"

"Every single one."

"Even 8-tracks?"

"Even 8-tracks."

"Why would she do that?"

Grandpa shrugged and that was that.

While watching Grandpa's favorite show, *Hee Haw*, on the 13" black and white Magnavox setup in the corner of the kitchen one evening, Johnny Cash made his appearance and I was *mesmerized*. When I asked Grandpa if he'd buy me a Johnny Cash record (since all of his were unavailable thanks to the mystery hoarder lady in *MA-ZURA*), he huffed, "Johnny's my cousin and we don't like each other!" He stood up and turned the TV off.

Wide-eyed I gasped, "*You're* related to Johnny Cash? Wow!"

I never got my Johnny Cash record and mentioning Johnny in casual conversation wasn't smiled upon.

One day Grandpa handed me a well-traveled (translation: beat-to-hell) acoustic guitar and said, "I bought this for *you* today, Son."

I have to think that I disappointed him and that whatever investment he made in me via that guitar went to waste. He never showed me how to play it and I wasn't musically gifted. The guitar sat in the corner gathering dust.

That was 35 years ago and I've come to the following conclusions:

Adam "Sonny" Sanders was never a famous musician and wasn't related to Johnny Cash.

He couldn't teach me the guitar because he couldn't read music. My step-grandpa played *his* brand of country/blues and made it up as he went along. And he was musically gifted.

I can still hear his voice in my mind and, for that, I'll always be grateful:

I said-a any ole time yer feelin' lonely . . . any ole time, yer feeling blue . . . just know baby . . . I'll be there . . . I'll be there for you.

No, Sonny wasn't famous but he was my grandpa and that's good enough for me.

To all you public nose blowers . . .

I've never understood the three camps of people who blow their noses in public.

Camp One are the people who toot their noses like a trumpet and sometimes I *seriously* wonder if there's an elephant two cubicles over. I literally stop whatever I'm doing and wait for the proboscis to wander over my cubicle wall in search of a peanut.

For as bad as the trumpeters are, Camp Two nose blowers are worse. These are the people who are doggedly-determined to expend that gelatinous chunk of mucous clogging the nasal cavity.

[Sidenote: While researching Nasal Congestion Relief on ehow.com, the page has a link to "How to Frontside Nose Grind on a Skateboard" and "Oven Cooking Time for an Unstuffed Turkey." Am I the only one confused here?]

Where were we?

Oh yeah, the sound of gelatinous mucous in motion. For Chrissake, am I the only one grossed out by this?

Camp Three are the gifted few who incorporate *both* sounds. Sometimes at the same time starting with the mucous flow and ending with the triumphant toot.

Sonny Sanders fell in Camp Three. He'd pull out a white handkerchief from his overalls, blow forcefully, fold the rag in a perfect square, and *put it back in his pocket*.

OK, it *was* cotton and I suppose Grandma washed it from time to time but, good Christ, it grossed me out every time. The thing was a crunchy yellow so I'm thinking it wasn't washed nearly enough.

Public nose blowing, for me, is akin to public expulsion of gases through the rectum. Yes, people, I'm talking about flatulence, breaking wind, passing gas . . . *farts!* Why don't people rear back and let loose their backside discharge in public? What's the difference between that and trumpeting the snot out of your nose?

And farting has a colorful history!

Chaucer wrote about farts in his *Canterbury Tales*.

Shakespeare made use of the act in *The Comedy of Errors*.

It is reported that one early version of Act 3, Scene 1 of *Julius Caesar* included the line, "Doth not Brutus bootless kneel and pass triumphant wind from thine backside after that delicious lunch of brie and grape leaves?" Of course, we know that most of this line ended up lost for eternity somewhere along the way. Which is a damn shame if you ask me.

[I *am* kidding here.]

And lest we not forget the 19th century Frenchman, Joseph Pujol, who made a living blowing out candles from across the room and making music with his, uh, *backside prowess.*

But why stop with that sphincter?

How about belching? Why don't we make use of our upper esophageal sphincter? Babies do it in public so why can't adults? Hell, my brother Lorne can belch his way through an entire conversation.

And so I ask the public nose blowers again. *What the hell?* What unwritten rule makes it OK to blow snot–the disgusting sound forced upon the quiet masses in cubicles, libraries, grocery aisles and during performances of the Seattle Symphony–and yet, it's *not* OK to blow ass or belch out loud?

Where is that written, people? *Where?*

That thing has *how many* calories?

God bless the Hostess Corporation, makers of Ding Dongs, Cup Cakes, HoHos, SnoBalls, and the venerable Twinkie. For as glorious as these five treats were, my personal favorite was the simply-named Fruit Pie. And while there were seven flavors (name them if you can!), for me back in the day, there was only one:

Lemon.

Don't Fight with the Garden Hose

I am reminded on the Hostess Brands webpage that "The Magician" was the official mascot of the Hostess Fruit Pie family. The Magician was no David Copperfield, that's for sure–he wasn't successful in making calories disappear and he couldn't save Hostess from bankruptcy. We'll get to the calories shortly but it makes me wonder if the two are related.

In the 2004 documentary, *Super Size Me*, a normal guy named Morgan Spurlock goes on a quest to eat nothing but McDonald's, three times a day for 30 continuous days. Morgan's objective is to document how detrimental fast food can be to one's physical and psychological well-being.

You seriously gotta love the guy for putting his liver at risk for posterity's sake.

One scene is sickening in the most hilarious of ways.

Morgan sits in his car trying to conquer a Double Quarter Pounder with Cheese, a super-sized portion of fries, and a 42-ounce Coke.

[One self-imposed rule was if the counter-person asked if he'd like to Super Size That, he *had* to say yes.]

As he turns a darker shade of green with each bite, he narrates how uncomfortable the expansion of his stomach feels.

Cold sweat runs down his face.

In no time at all, Morgan hurls it out the window in a series of loud splats. I watched this on a plane and, literally, had to bury my face in my hands to avoid the wrath of the people around me.

Why do I mention this in the context of the innocent Hostess Lemon Fruit Pie?

Let's stack up that tasty little pastry against that other staple of our youth, the McDonald's Big Mac:

Calories:
- Lemon Pie: 490
- Big Mac: 540

Carbs:
- Lemon Pie: 69 grams
- Big Mac: 45 grams

Sugar:
- Lemon Pie: 38 grams
- Big Mac: 9 grams

Fat:
- Lemon Pie: 22 grams
- Big Mac: 29 grams

Sodium:
- Lemon Pie: 420 mgs
- Big Mac: 1,040 mgs

Morgan Spurlock's movie is funny to me because *I am that guy* when it comes to eating a Big Mac. About twenty years ago, my body declared war on McDonald's.

Go ahead and just try to eat a Big Mac. I double dog dare you.

I can't do it without the immediate threat of liquid fire shooting out of both ends–past the esophageal sphincter and, well, that *other* sphincter. The Big Mac and Lemon Hostess Fruit Pie–symbols of a youth I no longer enjoy.

Gone are the days when I could bite off a corner of the pie, oblivious to the calorie, carb, sugar, fat, and sodium count and suck–suuuuuuck–out that lemony-snot goodness. In the ignorance of my youth and with an iron stomach, I owned that freaking pie. I could even eat it after downing that obnoxious Big Mac. *Hell, pass some fries while you're at it! Side salad? No thanks!*

One thousand thirty calories? HA.

Puking my guts out? I think not.

But gone are those days for *this* old guy.

And I say that with a sigh.

Sigh.

Other Tom Harveys

The great thing about having two somewhat-common names is that there are other wonderfully awesome Tom Harveys in the world.

Hey, if you're ever in the Cincinnati area with your four-legged little buddy, take a stroll over to the Tom Harvey Memorial Dog Park in Blanchester, Ohio. As quoted in the Clinton County, Ohio News Journal, "It's the best in the Cincinnati area." My late namesake won the Blanchester Businessman of the Year Award. Clearly he was one smart cookie!

Speaking of smart cookies, the physicist Albert Einstein has ties to a different Tom Harvey–but I'm fairly certain Einstein didn't know the guy. *This* Tom Harvey, Doctor Harvey to you and I, was the pathologist who autopsied the father of modern physics. Apparently the good doctor carried around slices of Einstein's brain for his own personal research.

What dedication!
What commitment!
What a freak!

Returning to Ohio for the last of the spotlighted Tom Harveys, east of Cleveland and four hours from the dog park, sits Thomas Harvey High School. Just an Uncle Rico's throw from Lake Erie, the Red Raiders look like they've got it going on. Hall of Fame Coach Don Shula (who I met in the Memphis airport a few years back–and I got a picture to prove it!) is an alum so I say, *Beat the crap out of the rival Riverside Beavers! Dam those beavers! Dam those beavers!*

There are *other* Tom Harveys, past and present, in the world and to them I say, *Make me look good with that awesome name of yours!*

Leave it to the automotive industry!

If I learned nothing else my freshman year of high school, I know the colors of the spectrum thanks to the stubby-fingered teaching of Mr. Forrest. Every single rainbow since the dawn of time is arranged thus: red, orange, yellow, green, blue, violet. These are our six primary colors but, because we're humans and don't believe in keeping things simple, we have created many, *many* color variations.

My favorite color is blue–midnight blue to be exact–and thanks to Foreigner's former lead singer, Lou

Gramm, for pointing out that life is either "midnight blue or cherry red!"

When it came time to jettison the 17-miles-to-the-gallon Toyota Tundra, I called up the local Mini Cooper dealer.

"Got any blue Mini's?" I asked.

"You want Ice, Kite, Lightning, or Reef?"

"Huh? Blue. You got any blue Mini's?"

"You want Ice Blue, Kite Blue, Lightning Blue, or Reef Blue?"

Good grief, we bought a white Mini–Pepper White, to be exact–and passed over Iced Chocolate, Spice Orange, and Highclass Gray (to name just a few).

Susan drives a green Prius; correction, it's a *seafoam* Prius. And if you were to go Prius shopping nowadays, you would choose from Sea Glass Pearl, Nautical Blue Metallic, Winter Gray Metallic, Blizzard Pearl, Classic Silver Metallic, Black, Barcelona Red Metallic, and Black Cherry Pearl.

Clearly, the automotive industry can't stay within a simple color palette. But I do like how *Barcelona Red Metallic* rolls off the tongue.

Just because you *can* doesn't mean you *should*

When my oldest brother, Lorne, and I get together, God help us.

Literally, God please help us.

Daredevil David, the middle brother, invited us to his motocross race in Reno. The plan was to fly into Sacramento and *vamoose* in the motor home from the

Sacramento airport to the Reno fairgrounds–another Arenacross on the agenda. This was years before *The Big Crash* of chapter 13.

Lorne flew in from Walla Walla and, there we were, the bookend brothers at the SeaTac airport. Lorne's grin widened when I told him we were in First Class for the 90-minute flight.

There *is* a drink limit somewhere in the Alaska Airline regulations, but as the charm poured out (and the drinks poured in), our flight attendant cut us some major slack.

Before we left the gate, we had a nice little Gin and Tonic.

Ding. We've reached 10,000 feet and portable electronics are now approved.

Gin and Tonic #2.

Twenty minutes into the flight.

Gin and Tonic #3.

"So, Lorne, wasurepleasue?"

I'm *such* a lightweight.

"Let's have some bloodys."

"Oh, Miss?"

"You know, there *is* a maximum drink allotment," she whispered.

The fact that our flight attendant was whispering to the cheesedicks in 1A and 1C was encouraging.

"Ya know, as soon as we land in Sack-eramento, I'm taking *my buddy* here to the altar. He's gettin' married *tonight!* He's hours away from a new life . . . and . . . a new wife! Hey, that (*burp*) rhymes!"

Lorne looked at me like I was as smart as the Tom Harvey who carried around slices of Einstein's brain.

She smiled like we were a couple of mischievous ten-year-olds and raised her eyebrows.

Translation: *What'll it be?*

"Two Bloody Marys," Lorne said, "each."

By my sober math, we're talking five drinks in the course of 45 minutes. And that kind of drinking works when you're comfortably seated and simply trying not to piss yourself.

And so we sat, giggling.

As the plane began its descent, our attentive attendant offered up one more gratuitous libation. Lorne knew just want we needed.

"Bailey's and coffee."

Once we landed, my ability to negotiate a straight line was shot to hell so we serpentined from the jetway to the curb. Brother Dave, oblivious to the activity of the last 90 minutes, had no idea we'd be completely worthless for the entire trip.

I passed out (something I hadn't done since my first attempt at being an exotic dancer [as chronicled in *The Eighties*, on sale at your friendly Amazon.com!]) then summarily blew chunks at the first moment of regaining consciousness. (And, no, Chunks isn't the name of a dog.)

"Where are we?" I croaked.

"We're in a casino parking lot. Lorne went in to play blackjack."

Lorne *was* from Eastern Washington so I give him credit for his drinking ability.

Thirty minutes later he stumbled back to the RV, forty dollars lighter and still drunk off his keister. In fact, he had *added* alcohol to his severely-compromised system.

The next day I sat in the stands at the Reno Fairgrounds nursing what was, perhaps, the worst headache in the history of mankind.

And so I say:

Just because you *can* get hammered in First Class doesn't mean you should!

Just because you *can* blow your nose in a library doesn't mean you should!

Just because you *can* do something doesn't mean you should.

Make a note of it.

Conquering *The Omega Man*

As you learned in Chapter 6, the Charlton Heston sci-fi/horror movie, *The Omega Man*, left an impression on me as an 8-year-old. At the time, I remember crying for Mom to come and turn on the bathroom light–afraid that a nocturnal, mutant freak may be lurking behind the door. Many *sleep-with-the-lights-on-nights* ensued.

Oh, Meatball was *not* happy about this.

Let's face it, *The Omega Man* has scarred my psyche since 1976.

It is now 2013, however, and I finally decided that enough was enough. It was time to face my fear so I ordered the blu-ray for the new *blu-ray player setup in the bedroom*. And there the movie sat in a small stack that included *Soylent Green, Logan's Run,* and *The Princess Bride*. How's *that* for diversity?

I didn't watch it right away and, lo and behold, I actually had a nightmare about pale-faced nocturnal freaks chasing me down a dark alley. The memories of my 8-year-old self had managed one last hurrah for the now-45-year-old. Good grief, the madness must end!

So with Susan asleep and the two Shiba Inu's sprawled out to maximum girth one Saturday night, I loaded *The Omega Man* and went for broke. At worst, I figured Susan would turn the bathroom light on for me if I asked nicely.

The blu-ray didn't waste any time at all–didn't even load up the menu–and the first scene played out exactly as I remember it: Charlton driving the deserted and newspaper-strewn streets of downtown Los Angeles. Christ, who was his dentist and, seriously, did they not have teeth-whitening products in the '70s?

I drew the covers up in a ball around me, displacing my overweight Shiba Inu, Taz, who snorted his disapproval but watched the screen from his horizontal position. (I refer to him as a "who" since he doesn't know he's a dog. He actually thinks he's a very small fat man.)

As the movie played, I relaxed my grip on the covers and came to view *The Omega Man*, and my very existence, in a much different light. Was this a sci-fi/horror movie or a comedy? For the most part, the movie didn't make a lot of sense! Let me share the obvious:

Charlton finds himself the only "normal" person in a city populated by two dozen plague victims. Two dozen white-faced, lesioned-out people who 1) shop at the same Sunglasses Hut with their clunky, mirrored shades, 2) shop at the same Black Cloaks Are Us Superstore, and 3) refuse to use modern weapons against him. Since "The Family," as they call themselves, seem hell-bent on torturing our hero by mostly wailing at him from outside his window at night, it would only take a week or two for our military scientist hero to snipe them all from the comfort of his upper floor balcony.

Take a shot of Crown Royal. Splatter a nocturnal freak's melon.

And repeat.

Nah, that would be too easy.

Charlton, instead, cruises town during the day shooting out windows. And for the future five time president of the National Rifle Association, he was a really, *really* lousy shot.

Lo and behold, our hero *is* captured and taken to–where was that, the Great Western Forum?–to be burned at the stake. Since the freaks are light-sensitive, the floodlights of the arena blind them into cowering, helpless wimps. Once Charlton's binds are cut by a guy who looks like a young Billy Jack, the lights are extinguished and the chase is on. Now, seriously, why were the lights turned *off*? In the post-apocalyptic future, were they *that* concerned about energy conservation?

I damn near woke Susan laughing at the racial zinger that I'm convinced is ad-libbed based on the expressions of everyone in the scene. I won't spoil it but it involves the word "spooked."

Fast forward to the ending and the miraculous spear throw from the leader of the bad guys. (But are they *really* that bad? I think they're mostly misunderstood. Can't we all just get along?) King Freako zings a bull's-eye at 50 yards and a 45 degree downward angle. With that kind of skill, I seriously hope that guy tried out for the track and field events at the 1972 Summer Olympics!

The next day I found myself bustling with energy and realized that *The Omega Man* had been a weight on my shoulders for most of my life. It was one of those movies that always haunted me in the recesses of my mind. I faced my fear by watching the movie from the perspective of my adulthood. The fear and anxiety from the 8-year-old lurking around my brain disappeared completely. Hell, *The Omega Man* is a freaking comedy!

And, you know what, I like the movie.

A lot.

I think I'll watch it again.

Now, who's with me?

Keep turning the corner, Bryan(s)

I happen to know *two* guys who spell their common names in the uncommon fashion, *Bryan*. This next lesson applies equally to them, though they don't know each other. In fact, one's on the East Coast and the other's on the West.

The year was 1997 and I was in the throes of depression.

Unemployed.

My girlfriend just broke up with me.

Man, I was in the *dumps.*

After begging everyone I knew in the business for a job, I was out of favors. This only meant one thing. I was going to have to move.

My break finally came but it was one tough pill to swallow. Stephen (the dude from Chapter 10) called and said a job was opening up in Seattle. Out of local options and with a feeling of excitement *and* dread, I flew up for an interview. A few days later an offer of employment came in the mail and there I was staring at God's one and only path:

Relocating from the small town I called home.

A place where I felt safe.

A place where I could work on patching things up with my girlfriend.

A place where unemployment was going on nine months.

A place where I was utterly miserable.

No, I *had* to go. God's instructions were blatantly clear:

You will stop playing Nintendo 64 all day long!

You will stop making potato and leek soup every day for your roommates!

You will stop answering the door and turning away the Schwan's frozen food guy who has special pricing 'but only if you order today!'

And you will stop feeling sorry for your unemployed ass as I've lined you up with a cool job with cool people in a cool new place.

I signed the offer of employment and loaded my crappy little Saturn with every scrap of clothing that would fit.

On Leaving Day, I made two stops on my way out of town.

First to my ex-girlfriend which only made me feel worse. I kissed her soft lips, burst into tears, and left her standing on her front porch with her arms crossed.

Second to my dear friend, Paul. One of my ex-coworkers at the hospital who I loved and admired like a dad.

"So, this is it, huh?" he asked. He gripped my shoulder with his strong hand.

My eyes flooded with tears, again, which began spilling onto his living room carpet. I could only nod and look at the floor.

Paul's wife, Alice, watched from the kitchen, a motherly smile on her face.

"It's going to be fine," he said. "This is a good thing. A real good thing."

He wrapped his arms around me and I cried into his shirt.

"I'll be all alone," I sobbed. "I don't know a single person in Seattle. I don't really want to go."

He broke the embrace and held me at arm's length.

"Listen here, Tom. You won't be alone for long. You'll find the love of your life when you least expect it."

"In fact," he continued, "*you will turn a corner and there she'll be*." Alice nodded enthusiastically.

"How do you know?"

"*I know.*"

He gave me a shake and I smiled.

They walked me to the curb and the tears came back as I left my friend and the town I called home.

Paul, indeed, was right about what he said that day. Without even trying, Susan and I found each other. *I turned the corner and there she was*, just as he described.

And so I say to my two Bryans, both dealing with life's loves and losses:

Keep turning the corner my friends.

Keep turning the corner because the loves of your lives are out there.

Trust me on this one.
I know.

> Garden Hose Lesson Learned:
> Lotta lessons still to be learned, hosers!

1 9

Tom the terrorist

[Note: This is the one chapter Susan asked me not to write. And while she didn't expressly forbid it, the principles of Chapter 2 loosely apply here. If you've recovered from the emotion of Chapter 16 (and if you didn't cry, what are you a f---ing Vulcan?!), I hope that this chapter counteracts it with a good laugh. Once again, I can't make this stuff up–I'm not that imaginative.]

• • •

Susan and I flew into Sacramento in February, 2012 for the annual birthday weekend since my birthday, David's birthday, and Chloe's birthday are within eight days of each other. After playing with my gag gift for all of ninety seconds, I forgot all about it. Four days later when Susan packed our bags to head home, little did I know the button to the bureaucratic machine had been firmly mashed.

• • •

Susan and I have enjoyed MVP Gold status on Alaska Airlines since 2001, meaning that we fly at least 40,000 miles a year. That's not the easiest thing to do, by the way. Two years ago we received a letter from Alaska Air stating that, as elite flyers, we qualified for the "TSA Express Line." This kind of promotion–where you don't have to take off your shoes or show everyone your tiny fluids in a Zip-loc bag–is exciting stuff.

Here's one way to get kicked off this list.

• • •

You know those mysterious doors in airports? The gray, non-descript doors with random numbers such as A1492 and K11? They're seemingly everywhere in the larger airports and every time I see one with a small number (ie, M44), I have an instinct to cry out, "M44? You sunk my battleship!" I never do since that would draw unwanted attention from the stern-looking airport cops.

There is a severe shortage of humor in airports these days and, in the Sacramento International Airport, a severe lack of common sense. I found out what was behind those doors thanks to that objectionable item Susan so conveniently packed in *my* bag on that fateful day in February, 2012.

On this day, Susan zipped through a different line and called out that she'd meet me at the gate. I nodded. Successfully passing the *Full Body Yes We Can See Your Junk (But It's OK Because We're In Another Room)* scanner–the one since jettisoned because, yes, indeed, junk can be seen–the only thing keeping me from joining Susan was my carryon bag making its way through the x-ray machine.

And behind those mysterious doors lie dozens of TSA agents who look exactly like Jonah Hill (and if you don't know who that is, go out to www.imdb.com because you need the visual). Because as I stood patiently–*ignorantly*–waiting for my bag, they came streaming out like wasps out of a nest. Suddenly there were a dozen TSA-Jonah-Hills crowded around the x-ray monitor. Oh, they were excited! I thought, *Whoever owns the bag they're looking at is screwed! Now, where's my bag?*

In the weakest, most non-confrontational voice I've ever heard from a member of the sex of which I belong, the Jonah Hill nearest me asked, "Can I see your boarding pass again? Oh, and your driver's license?"

I handed it over thinking, *This doesn't sound good.*

"You don't, by the way, happen to have *NUNCHUCKS* in your bag, do you?" he asked. The offending word was emphasized at twice the volume of the rest of the question. He even did a little genuflect for good measure.

"Huh? Oh, that? No, it's a gag gift. Just a toy. I just had a birthday. Look at my license if you don't believe me."

He didn't look.

The eleven wide-eyed Jonahs crowded around the monitor started to spread out in a wide circle around me. Had there been a red panic button–you know, one that dropped Jackie Chan and a cargo net from the ceiling–one that let a dozen pissed off, snarling German Shepherds loose with the overhead cry of "Abschuss! Biss! ReiBen Sie seine verdammten Balle ab!"–one of those guys definitely would have hit it. [That's *Kill! Bite! Rip his f---ing balls off!* in German. Thank you freetranslation.com.]

"We're gonna have to call a LEO."

"Uh, am I supposed to know what that is?"

"Law. Enforcement. Officer."

"You're going to call the cops? Hell, you can keep the thing. I have a flight to catch."

"They're already on their way," he said. Then with a little more assertion, "And you're not going *anywhere*."

I laughed at the guy–which isn't recommended.

Less than thirty seconds later, the first Sacramento Deputy Sheriff skidded his mountain bike to a stop leaving an impressive black mark on the polished white floor. As he dismounted, he clicked off the flashing blue light. Anyone watch Reno 911? If you do, then describing this guy as a black Lieutenant Dangle has meaning. Short shorts. Bicycle helmet. Tube socks. High-tops. Porn 'stauche. Oh, this guy was imposing.

Again, I laughed at the absurdity–which, again, isn't recommended.

Clicking his helmet off, this black Superhero shoved his face into mine–seriously breaching the Personal Private Perimeter–so that our noses practically touched.

"Something funny here?" he snorted.

"Funny that the TSA thinks two pieces of plastic covered by an inch of foam requires calling a, what's the term?"

I paused for dramatic effect, "Oh, a *LEO*."

Super Deputy took a step back and almost stepped on the foot of the largest human being I have ever seen. Sacramento Sheriff Deputy Number Two had arrived. A cross between Andre The Giant and Ed "Too Tall" Jones, this guy had to be seven feet tall and three hundred pounds–and the guy wasn't fat, he was just *massive*. *This* guy was imposing.

"What do we got?" he asked.

"This guy's carrying nunchucks!" Dangle said.

The hushed crowd of about two hundred people, mostly on the wrong side of the now-forgotten scanners, watched intensely. You could hear a pin drop.

"If you'd bother looking at it, you'll see that it's a toy. It's not like a, you know . . ." I cocked my right thumb back but didn't dare discharge my index finger at the big guy.

[Following the lesson learned from Ben Stiller in *Meet The Parents* (that is, don't say "bomb" on a plane), I figured you don't say the word "gun" to the biggest airport cop in the universe.]

While this was happening, the nasally TSA guy had copied all of my driver's license information on the back of a diagram of fluids in a Zip-loc. He looked up at the two deputies and stammered, "Can't find the form so I just grabbed the nearest piece of paper." He handed my license to the big boy who promptly disappeared behind one of those mysterious gray doors. Dangle stood by in the attack position–waiting, hoping, praying–I'd make a sudden move. I didn't.

I smiled at Dangle which seemed to piss him off all the more. What the hell else could I do?

"Are you a certified Martial Arts Instructor?" he growled.

"No."

"Don't you know you need a license to have nunchucks in the state of California?"

"No, I didn't know that. How about toy nunchucks? Did you need a license for those? I have a squirt gun at home. Do I need a license for that too?"

[I quickly determined that saying "gun" to the little LEO wasn't going to degrade the situation anymore than it was.]

Before he could answer, my cell phone rang. Holding up a finger, I said, "Sorry. Gotta take this." If the guy had been a teapot he would have blown at that moment.

"Where are you? They're boarding the plane!" Susan exclaimed.

"Oh, we're having fun down here at security. The LEOs have been called."

"What's a LEO?"

I turned to the TSA guy. "See! My wife doesn't know what a LEO is either!"

Speaking back in the phone, "It's a Law Enforcement Officer. I have one about two feet from me at this very moment. Dave's little gag gift has agitated quite a lot of people here."

"I'll be right there!" Click.

This wasn't actually the truth because Susan never came within a hundred feet of where I stood–the epicenter of a circle of TSA Jonah Hills and one look-at-me-I'm-suddenly-important-LEO. She stood in the main terminal alternating hands on hips, hands in the air. I shrugged.

Ten minutes later Neanderthal LEO reappeared and with a hint of disappointment said, "This guy doesn't have a record." And then the coup de grace of coup de graces. Holding up the toy nunchucks, the big fella asked, "You want this back?"

"You're offering it back to me now? No, I do not want it back! Can I go now?"

"Yeah, you can go. We'll destroy it for you."

"You do that."

I grabbed my bag and hurried toward Susan as the TSA guy called after me, "You'll be getting a letter from the TSA and, possibly a fine! Hey! Possibly a fine! Did you hear me?"

I held up the peace sign but didn't turn around. Never in my life have I wanted to lower my index finger more than I did at that moment.

• • •

Four months later, the letter arrived. And because I *do* want to fly again in this big country of ours, I'll leave out the names to protect the dumbasses.

Citing TSA regulation 1540.111(a)(1), I was summarily scolded for possession of a "prohibited item (1 Nunchucks) discovered during the screening process at the Sacramento International Airport." This Warning Notice from the US Department of Homeland Security *adequately addressed the incident* though it didn't resolve "any other federal, state, or local criminal proceeding that may have been brought against you."

Gee, thanks fellas.

To which I responded, in writing, that I "summarily rejected the facts as presented" in my Warning Notice. Citing dictionary.com, nunchucks are defined as "an Oriental hand weapon for defense against frontal assault, consisting of two foot-long *hardwood* sticks joined by a chain or thick cord that stretches to body width." I pointed out that the toy in my bag did not meet this definition. I also made the point that if toy nunchucks were illegal in California, "law enforcement would have their hands full apprehending tens of thousands of 10-year-old boys." I also noted that I was confused that two pieces of plastic covered by an inch of foam was more lethal than, say, *the steel knife and fork Alaska Airlines hands out in their first class cabin! You know, the cabin nearest the freaking cockpit!* (I didn't say *freaking*, FYI.)

With enough practice with *the toy* I might be able to knock a drink out of someone's hand but that's the extent of the damage I think I could do. Pry apart the cheap chain and you've got yourself two foam batons. Are two foam batons prohibited items? It's so confusing.

I concluded with the following:

"If a Written Notice is warranted in this matter, I expect it to reflect the facts: the offending item was, in fact, NOT 'nunchucks' by definition. Rather, the item was a facsimile of nunchucks–an item perfectly legal in every US state." I cc'd Janet Napolitano, Secretary of Homeland Security, for good measure, but am still waiting on her response.

Six weeks later the guy who lacks all humor in his life responded with, "We're not changing our documentation. Our 'travel attorney' said so."

To which I responded, "Please provide me with all documents from your 'travel attorney' because I am very interested in knowing how two pieces of plastic covered by one inch of foam is a lethal weapon under federal TSA definition." It's been over a year and I'm still awaiting the response.

That was then. This is now.

I've flown out of SeaTac at least a dozen times since the incident in Sacramento. Interestingly enough, I'm 0 for 12 when it comes to using the TSA Express Line. See, even with the extra special designation, there's *supposed* to be an element of chance that even the designated elite flyers get kicked over to the regular security line. They scan the barcode on your boarding pass. If the light turns green, you're good to go! If the light turns red, you get jettisoned over to the regular security line.

I've seen red every time since February, 2012.

Susan's seen green every time.

I guess that evens it out, statistically speaking.

> Garden Hose Lesson Learned:
> Fighting the TSA with logic is like
> urinating in the wind.
> There is a feeling of relief but
> you're going to end up getting pissed on in the end.

20

What every 14-year-old should know

Mom died.

If there's a magic pill to ease the pain I'd be an addict. With every breath I take, my heart reminds me she's gone. What's a guy to do without his mother?

Here's one thing I did.

I established the Patricia Ann Harvey Memorial Nursing Scholarship, awarded each year to graduates of my high school, Monache, who are going into the nursing program at Porterville Junior College.

[I went to Monache High School. Mom went to Porterville College. Go to YouTube and type in Patricia Ann Harvey Memorial Nursing Scholarship 2009 and you can watch the first presentation where I ad-lib a couple jokes and have to stop, twice, to fight back tears.]

Going strong since 2009, this scholarship gives me the opportunity to return to Porterville, California and look around the high school halls of my youth. Though it's May when I go back, I am reminded of Charles Dickens and *A Christmas Carol*.

But it's not the Ghosts of Christmas who haunt me. My ghost has long brown hair and a curly moustache. It wears a red Le Tigre shirt and Levis 501 blue jeans. It's the Ghost of my Teenage Youth.

I've just closed my locker, slipped a note in Betsy's locker (since mine had *two* from her) and am hurrying to 7th period English for the College Bound.

I want to call out to that blur. I want to talk to him.

I blink and there's no one there. In fact, the lockers are gone too.

I look at the grassy patch where Jaime Smith *tried* to kick my 14-year-old ass. Unprovoked, he stormed off and I only had to swallow my pride (and, thankfully, no teeth).

I blink again and there's no one there.

I look at the entrance to the cafeteria and my prom date, Kellie, and I are making our grand entrance. Her green, shimmery cocktail dress is striking against my white tuxedo with tails. My hair is slicked back (very Steven Seagal-like even though we wouldn't know Steven Seagal for another two years); her hair is woven with pretty pink and white flowers. The crowd parts for us and we can't stop smiling.

I blink and those two kids have long since disappeared.

I gaze at the stage where David and I were band mates, lip-syncing our way to temporary rock star status during the annual "Battle of the Bands."

But I'm 45-years-old and decades removed from these images in my mind.

The scholarship recipients sit in chairs on the stage looking down at their proud parents. There's a vibe to the place–the excitement and anticipation of these college-bound kids–but I'm a stranger here. To them, this is simply a cafeteria. To me, this is *sacred ground.*

To a scattering of applause, I take the stage when my name is called. My heart races in anticipation. My first impulse is to turn around and ask, "*Well?* Was it the best four years of your life or what?" I fight this urge because I think they'd look at each other and whisper, "Who is this whack job? Isn't he here to present a scholarship like the rest of the adults here? I hope he makes it quick."

Principal Smithey allows me extra time since he knows it's a 1,000-mile journey for me to be here. I appreciate the consideration to stray from the two-minute allotment. (I average twelve minutes, *ha!*)

Seniors Now, Marauders Forever!

This was the motto of the class of '86 and I share that I stole the slogan and modified it from a T-shirt I saw during a recruiting visit to USC. (Not sure how I'd feel about being a *Trojan* forever.)

Carpe Diem!

The crowd relives my favorite scene from *Dead Poet's Society*. The parents nod their heads and smile.

Yeah, it's an honor to stand in front of these graduating high school seniors.

A true privilege.

• • •

Don't Fight with the Garden Hose

I leave that night thinking *there's something missing*.

Giving them a pep talk with two weeks left of their high school experience is *too late*. These kids need instructions *before* their high school journey begins.

And, thus, here is *my* Top 10 list of what every 14-year-old kid should know:

1) High school is a magical four year window. Make the absolute most of it! Play sports! Join clubs! *Get involved!*
2) If you *don't* get involved, someone else will! If you don't run for Student Council, *someone else will!* If you don't try out for the Cheer Squad, *someone else will!*
3) You're going to see the same people every day for four years so don't be a jerk. Be nice and make friends.
4) Don't tie yourself down in a relationship. I have friends who look back on high school with dread because every memory is attached to their ex-boyfriend/girlfriend.
5) To quote my brother David: "Enjoy yourself but kick ass in school." Life after high school can be *so* much easier, in the form of scholarships and grants, if you stretch for that A.
6) Bruce Springsteen's got it right–these *are* your *Glory Days* and they *will* pass you by (in the wink of a young girl's eye).
7) Don't look back and think, *I should have–I could have*. To quote Nike, *Just Do It!*

8) Don't skip/ditch class. Enjoy *every high school day* as the irreplaceable gift that it is. Go to *every* football game and rally. Go to *every* school dance.
9) As you climb the high school ladder, be nice to those below you! After high school, it really won't matter that you were a year (or two or three) older than the classes that came after you.
10) Enjoy your youth because it doesn't last nearly long enough!

And there you have it. Nothing too earth shattering. You could even say these are simple words of common sense. And who would argue with instilling common sense into our next great generation?
Anyone?
Anyone?
Bueller?
Bueller?

> Garden Hose Lesson Learned:
> *Celebrate Youth! Celebrate!*
> *(Hey, isn't that a Rick Springfield song?)*

2 1

What's *your* personal mix tape?

The accounting term is *scrubbing the data*.

That is, keep scrutinizing the numbers; keep kicking the tires; keep digging for the answer. And, thus, I have an assignment for *you*. While you may think this will be easy, let me tell you, it's not. I've tried a variation of this exercise on Facebook and *each and every time*, people can't do it. I'll post something like, *Give me your favorite U2 song* and, invariably, people will list their top five. Why? Because it's *damn hard* to drill down to just one.

And so I say again, "Scrub the data! Drill down! Work for it."

Here's how it's going to go.

You're going to put down this book and it will *literally* take you weeks to come up with your personal mix tape. And when I say mix tape, I further challenge you to fifteen songs–fifteen, give or take, fits on a CD.

Not sixteen.

Not fifty.

Fifteen.

Think of it in these terms:

You're lying in the casket and you want to leave a memento to your family and friends. Something for Uncle Earl or Aunt Peggy to hand out at the after-funeral kegger that personifies *you*. Imagine the conversations people could have: "Wow, I can't believe Steve loved *Aqualung* so much, but now that I think about it, he really liked flute solos."

As for myself, I can almost hear future conversations long after I'm gone:

"Grandma Chloe, didn't you have a crazy uncle named Tom?"

"Yes, but we don't talk about him."

"Why, Grandma?"

"Well, for one, he base-jumped naked off the Empire State Building into the path of a New York City hover bus. It was an awful mess but, now that I think about it, it *was* a viral sensation for a few days back in 2052."

"Didn't he leave a mix tape? Oh, I just *have* to find out more about crazy Great Uncle Tom!"

Hey, the possibilities of thrilling future generations are endless.

But back to the task at hand.

Why is it so difficult to come up with fifteen (not sixteen, not fifty!) songs that, in their entirety, describe you and you alone?

Here's three good reasons:

One: The sheer mass of music that's out there.

If I were to click on my first iTunes song (Aaron Neville's *Rainy Night In Georgia*–the first song from his "Bring It On Home . . . the Soul Classics" CD), it would take TWENTY SEVEN days of 24/7 playing to arrive at ZZ Tops' *Legs*–the last song on their Greatest Hits CD. In between the soulful sound of Aaron Neville and the southern rock of ZZ Top lay 9,912 songs of *massive* diversity. We're talking AC/DC, James Taylor, Loverboy, Depeche Mode, April Wine, The B-52s, Barry White, Johnny Cash, David Bowie, INXS, John Mayer, Elvis, Gotye, Grandmaster Flash, Queen, Stabbing Westward, Vitamin String Quartet, and on and on and on.

And on.

Nearly fifty gigabytes of music.

And to think I gasped that our office server, nestled between dummy terminals in their monochrome splendor, had *one* gigabyte of storage. We've come a ways since 1990.

Two: Tastes change.

What could have been the favorite song of your youth may not even make the top 100 as an adult. Hmm. That probably holds true for any songs from the purple dinosaur. And what you loved last year could be a distant memory nowadays.

And, three: I can easily come up with fifteen songs *each* from INXS, U2, Loverboy, and Johnny Cash and proclaim, *These are all my favorite songs!*

Again, this isn't an easy exercise.

Keep scrubbing the data people!

Don't rush it.

But do consider which fifteen songs describe who you are as a person. Make your list of fifty. Keep dropping songs from it.

To follow is my personal mix tape. And let me dive into a thousand word dissertation for each of these songs explaining why I love them so.

On second thought, *nah*.

I'm not going to explain, defend, or otherwise justify the songs that, in their entirety, describe me as the unique individual I am. These are *my* songs for *my* reasons.

Scrubbed, sorted, and scrubbed some more.

Are there themes? Probably.

Is it diverse? Totally.

Do I love them? Completely.

So if you happen to end up at my after-funeral kegger, possibly after a base-jump gone wrong in the year 2052, fire up one of these songs and think, *Yeah, I can see that cheesewhiz loving this song.*

- Welcome To My World–Elvis Presley
- Wreck Of the Old 97–Johnny Cash
- Brain Damage–Pink Floyd
- Never Let Me Down Again–Depeche Mode
- Never Tear Us Apart–INXS
- Until the End Of the World–U2
- Another Saturday Night–Cat Stevens
- Undercover of the Night–The Rolling Stones
- Dreaming With My Eyes Open–Clay Walker
- Missing–Everything But The Girl
- Killing In The Name–Rage Against The Machine
- The Kid Is Hot Tonite–Loverboy
- But Anyway–Blues Traveler

- Uprising–Muse
- One Tree Hill–U2
- ~~Separate Ways (Worlds Apart)–Journey~~
- ~~No More Words–Berlin~~
- ~~Waiting For The End–Linkin Park~~
- ~~With A Little Help From My Friends–Joe Cocker~~
- ~~Sugar, Sugar–The Archies~~
- ~~Save Yourself–Stabbing Westward~~
- ~~Justify My Love–Madonna~~
- ~~Haunted–Poe~~
- ~~Pressure Drop–The Specials~~
- ~~The Obvious Child–Paul Simon~~
- ~~Pressure–Billy Joel~~
- ~~Mysterious Ways–U2~~
- ~~Lorca's Novena–The Pogues~~

Note: *Even by my own rules*, I couldn't do it. I couldn't come up with just fifteen songs.

Seriously, though. No Stevie Ray Vaughn, no David Bowie, no Elton John, no Chris Isaak?

Huh.

Oh, this is so hard!

You can apply this same line of thinking to your favorite concerts, your favorite CDs–hell, even your favorite Tom Cruise movies.

• • •

One word of caution if you're single and looking to impress a love interest. While springing a mix tape on the guy/gal *sounds* like a good idea, it can backfire on you.

Don't Fight with the Garden Hose

When I first moved to Seattle, I emailed a gal out of the blue with an invitation to lunch. She was a quasi-local celebrity–saw her picture in a local magazine–and decided I had nothing to lose. The worst she could have said was, "I'm married, thanks anyway," or "Thanks, but I don't have lunch with strangers who email me out of the blue." She said neither and agreed to have lunch one day. When I walked in the restaurant, my heart crashing in my chest, there she sat.

"Well," she smiled, "I thought my friends were playing a joke on me. Apparently they weren't."

"Yeah, well, I don't normally email strangers for lunch, but I just moved here and you're just so radiant in your picture."

She must have decided that I was being sincere since she motioned for me to sit down. We made it through lunch and she asked me to go kayaking on Lake Union that weekend. I immediately agreed even after she told me she was a collegiate rower.

The following weekend we kayaked around Lake Union for a few hours and as we said our goodbye, I sprung it on her:

The cassette tape.

(This was 1997 and I had asked if she had upgraded to a CD player for her Acura Integra. She hadn't.)

She hesitated like it was an engagement ring. This *personal* offering–from the guy who had taken her kayaking challenge without drowning himself–flustered her. I didn't even try giving her a smooch on the cheek, and this *was* the second date.

People who have read my memoir often marvel at my ability to remember the fine detail. I'm sorry to disappoint here, but I can only remember the *very first song* on the tape: the live version of *Bullet the Blue Sky* by U2.

Yeah, it's a political song.

And the Edge's guitar keeps the song . . . *edgy*.

A *bold, confident* song to be sure, but this "relationship" with the quasi-celebrity, pretty kayaking brunette called for boldness.

I called her a few days later.

"So, how'd you like the tape?" I asked. Damn, I was cool.

"I didn't like it at all."

Without a hint of humor, she was dead serious and it got worse from there.

"I don't think we should see each other again. Thanks for the lunch and for going kayaking. I'll just toss the tape if it's all the same to you. All right? Thanks again. Goodbye."

Click.

Now I'm not here to blame Bono and the boys for *Bullet the Blue Sky* but I am here to say, "Don't spring a mix tape on someone too soon 'cause you can end up bulleting yourself right out of the blue sky of the relationship!"

> Garden Hose Lesson Learned:
> What are your favorite things? Write them down and share them with friends and family!
> Oh, and use *Bullet the Blue Sky* with extreme caution!

2 2

Parting words from Arther Fox

193

know almost nothing about Mr. Arther Fox.

I do know that his final resting place is just a stone's throw from my grandparents' graves in Porterville's Vandalia Cemetery.

After some quick poking around on the internet, I learned that Mr. Fox died at the age of 49 in 1916. Meaning, at some point in the early part of the twentieth century, someone who loved him erected the marker that stands today.

The headstone is solid granite but the inscriptions of when he was born and when he died have long since disappeared.

I first noticed Arther (taking the liberty that we're on a first-name basis now) in 2006.

I was in Porterville for my 20th high school reunion and Vandalia Cemetery is always a stopping place when I visit the old hometown. If the grandparents *are* able to peer down from the clouds, I'm sure they appreciate the effort.

And there he lies, my boy Arther, an Iowan born March 4, 1867.

As a guy who studied history in college, I'm fascinated with the past and what happened during peoples' lifetimes. I like to apply the Ten Year Look Back.

As in:

Arther was 10-years-old in 1877.

Was he aware that the US was recovering from the Civil War and that war between the Sioux and US Calvary raged on the Great Plains?

Arther was 20 in 1887.

Had he heard of those new-fangled horseless carriage things called *automobiles* and did he try that drink *Coca-Cola*?

Arther was 30 in 1897.

Did he get caught up in the Klondike Gold Rush and give Alaska a go?

Arther was 40 in 1907.

Surviving into the new century, was he in California when the great San Francisco earthquake hit on April 18, 1906?

By 1916, Mr. Arther Fox, whose final resting place is under a non-descript granite marker in Porterville, California, was gone.

But how did he die?

I like to imagine him buying the farm while storming the trench, a heavy steel Brodie helmet firmly strapped to his chin, sawed-off shotgun shooting death and fire, Colt pistol on this hip, but the US didn't formally enter World War I until 1917 so that simply wouldn't be possible.

Maybe he perished in a fire after saving 30 orphans and a litter of kittens after feeding homeless people all day in a soup kitchen.

Maybe he walked out of a bar drunk off his ass and fell down an elevator shaft.

All of these questions and not a single answer.

Whatever he did during his life and *however* he died, I'm here to profess that he's left an indelible mark on *me*. And the day when I needed a bit of inspiration, I stumbled past a headstone. A headstone that read, simply:

Arther Fox. It Is Well.

And that is how Mr. Arther Fox, formerly of Iowa and dead these *97 years* touched me.

It Is Well.

Inspired me.

It *Is* Well.

Thank you, Arther.

Thanks for the reminder that . . .

It Is *Well*.

Garden Hose Lesson Learned:
Inspiration can come when you least expect it,
in the simplest of ways.

2 3

The Little Boy

I have been profoundly shaped by a story Mom read to me as a child. I often begged her to read it even though I could practically recite it word for word. Without pause, she would open the spiral bound book, flip to page 36, and read.

The story has haunted me over the years because I couldn't quite recall the title and didn't know the author's name. Since Mom died, the pain associated with the loss of the story was palpable.

As this book was in final development, Susan came across an envelope with the postmark March 14, 1988. It was from my mom to me at my college address in Canoga Park, California. In the envelope was the beautiful story by Helen E. Buckley entitled, "The Little Boy."

I wouldn't take a million bucks for the envelope with her handwriting and the enclosed story. As I read this now, I see myself on her lap and hear her voice as she reads the words.

Alas, as much as I wanted to reprint Ms. Buckley's wonderful story, repeated efforts at obtaining copyright permission from HarperCollins Publishing went ignored. Thus, out of respect for her work, I won't republish it here–but I do invite you to internet-search "The Little Boy by Helen E. Buckley" and read it.

2 4

Parting Thoughts

So here we are, together at the start and we've now come to the end. As I write these words, I imagine you reading them and my spirit soars. You've shared your most valuable commodity–*time*–with me and I am humbled.

Just like Burt Reynolds once said, "There ain't no Bandit without a Smokey!" Or something to that effect.

And there ain't no story to tell without someone to tell it to. So, again, thank you for *your* gift of time.

I was having coffee with Gloria Campbell of Sundial Press, LLC recently and told her about my *affliction*.

"I have writer's curse," I said. "I have to keep a pad of paper and pen on my nightstand because some nights my brain won't let me sleep. I've found I need to write things down in fear of forgetting them in the morning."

Gloria beamed.

"That's not the writer's curse. That's the writer's *blessing*."

So, Dear Reader, thank you for my writer's blessing. And . . .

Whether you loved this book (or *The Eighties*), or liked them, or just flat-out disliked them, let me tell you something you may not fully appreciate:

Authors read their Amazon reviews.

They matter.

So regardless of whether you like what I've written thus far, I would be honored to read your review(s): good, bad, or indifferent (and I've collected a little of all three so far).

And you know what else? If you email me at AuthorTomHarvey@gmail.com, I will email you back! That's a promise from a Cub Scout who won his Pinewood Derby in 1977. So that's a solid-gold promise.

Oh, and one more shout out to Lance Beauchamp. What a stud!

Susan, Big Man Lance, and Tamara

Books Read Along the Way

Left to Tell: Discovering God Amidst the Rwandan Holocaust by Immaculee Ilibagiza, Publisher: Hay House

Turning 44: . . . living beyond his years by Melissa Collier, Publisher: moxie mo, inc.

Delinquents In Paradise by Michael Schall Johnson, Publisher: Michael Schall Johnson

Fooling Houdini: Magicians, Mentalists, Math Geeks, and the Hidden Powers of the Mind by Alex Stone, Publisher: HarperCollins

Driving with Dead People: A Memoir by Monica Holloway, Publisher: Gallery Books

The Book of Vice: Very Naughty Things (and How to Do Them) by Peter Sagal, Publisher: Harper

Holding Breath: A Memoir of AIDS' Wildfire Days by Nancy Bevilaqua, Publisher: Nancy Bevilaqua

I Want it Now! A Memoir of Life on the Set of Willy Wonka and the Chocolate Factory by Julie Dawn Cole, Publisher: BearManor Media/Ocean View Publishing

Johnny Cash at Folsom Prison: The Making of a Masterpiece by Michael Streissguth, Publisher: Da Capo Press

Come What May by Rebecca Grant, Publisher: CreateSpace

Acknowledgements

First, I have to thank my wife, Susan, for always being the ray of sunshine that she is. While she literally runs circles around me with her boundless energy, this special lady lets me sleep in on the weekends and, occasionally, allows uninterrupted spans of X-Box gaming.

To my editor, Rhonda Stracener Maine, where no amount of appreciation is enough. Thank you for helping me see the forest through the trees and for your many, many edits and tweaks. Reading a draft manuscript *is* work and I can't thank you enough for your invaluable time, energy, enthusiasm, and guidance.

To my two friends, Carol Stafford Klatt and Nancy Bevilaqua, for your critically important organizational suggestions.

Thank you to my reading group: Paka Antle, Kris Dalbke Menneke, Brian Massey, Eric Simpson, Davi Tavares, Bryan Janeway, William Bryan Nix, and Gloria Campbell.

Thank you to my friend, Luciana Miller, self-proclaimed "Maker of the best meatballs in North America" thanks to "Nonno." And I can vouch for those meatballs! OMG, they are sublime! May she one day open Luciana's Ristorante in Bellingham, Washington. (Now accepting applications for franchises.)

Thank you to my nephew, Tommy, and three nieces, Hannah, Chloe, and Alli Kay. This foursome is the next generation of our small family and, despite the bumps in our lives, I have high hopes and aspirations for each of them. They're smart, good-looking, and confident. Not a bad combination!

To Ramiro, who trades dozens of funny and insulting texts with me on a daily basis. Here's my favorite from him:

"Coach Lambie loved to recite the vowels. One day he said, 'Tom you're up! Sweep right around the lockers and pick up all the dirty towels!'"

To Jim and Chaz, who *always* answer their phones when I call. I am truly blessed to have these two extra brothers in my life.

Lastly, thanks to Nancy Bevilaqua for sharing one of the most touching stories I have ever read: "Holding Breath: A Memoir of AIDS' Wildfire Days." While I've not met or even spoken to Nancy, we've traded books–and emails–and I'm proud to call her my friend. If you're ready for a heartfelt, touching story of compassion with real, imperfect people, I wholeheartedly recommend Nancy's book.

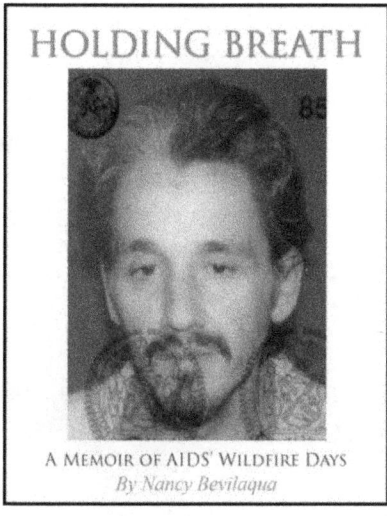

Tom
July 1, 2013

www.authortomharvey.com
www.facebook.com/86kicks
authortomharvey@gmail.com
Twitter handle: @authortomharvey

Tom will next try his hand in fiction. His third book, a supernatural thriller tentatively titled, "Mary Agnes," is in development.

Previously published in
"The Eighties: A *Bitchen* Time To Be a Teenager!"

Homage to a friend: the first of 290

It finally happened.

At work, the email subject line from Mike read, "Sad News." Clicking on the link brought me to the *Visalia Times Delta* obituaries:

Ryan Bernasconi, a Visalia police officer who fought cancer since 2001, died Tuesday. He was 39.

This makes Ryan the first death out of the Monache High School graduating class of 1986. The first that I'm aware of and I've kept dibs on the local hometown of Porterville through the local newspaper's online obituary. Morbid checking the online obituaries on a daily basis?

Perhaps, but somehow necessary.

As I sit here at my desk in Seattle, a thousand miles away from the Central Valley, I'm surprised at how sad this news makes me. I'm even more upset that my schedule won't allow me to attend his funeral two days from now. The funny thing is, I hadn't seen Ryan in twenty years.

Funnier still, when we first met, we didn't even like each other.

My family moved to Porterville when I was twelve. Showing up ten days into the sixth grade year, unfortunately for me, made me the "new kid." The morning of the very first day, Ryan and a couple of guys asked if I could throw a football. I smiled and said nothing. I think a few of them felt threatened by me as an unknown factor and soon Ryan and I had tension between us. He made a crack about my long hair and name: "Tom-*Ass*." I made a remark about his last name and he invited me to *meet him after school to settle some things*. I wasn't much of a fighter and replied, "I ride the bus." Within days, we were friends.

In junior high, we played on the flag football team together (we went 5-1) but Ryan was much more competitive than I was and went on to play basketball and baseball.

In high school, we tried out for the freshman football team. Tried out isn't exactly the truth, though, since everyone made the team. He quickly rose to quarterback, Number 15, while I struggled at the thankless position of defensive cornerback, Number 21. It didn't matter that we only won one game out of ten that year. We were fourteen years old. Competing, checking out the cheerleaders, getting to know all the new kids in the universe known as high school. We were immortal.

I can't say that Ryan and I were the best of friends through school. That simply wouldn't be the truth. But we did share the formidable years of twelve to eighteen and there's a lot of growing up in those six irreplaceable, precious years. He dated and ended up marrying Deanna Hall, a girl that I'd also known since the sixth grade. Together they radiated a genuine bond of love. When two good people come together, well, that's a pretty special thing.

So I sit here at my desk in Seattle, twenty years removed from those times and I mourn the loss of someone I haven't seen or talked to in twenty years. He had been battling cancer for five years and I didn't even know he was sick. The paper says he has a son, Tyler, twelve, and a daughter, Krysta, eight. Synovial Cell Sarcoma took their daddy away and here I sit claiming to have a right to my grief.

What gives *me* the right to feel sad?

I'd say that a person is nothing more than a collection of the memories he makes. I lost a rare someone who goes back to my junior high and high school days. This feeling of sadness is that with his death a part of me has died as well. How many guys have I known since I was twelve? The list is short and now it's one gaping hole shorter. It's a feeling of helplessness, knowing that his death by this terrible, rare cancer was nothing more than cruel randomness. Looking at his young, smiling face in our Senior Class yearbook, there was no way of knowing he wouldn't make it to our twenty-year reunion. It could have been any one of the two hundred ninety graduates of the class of 1986. For some reason, it was him.

I grieve for his children I've never met. I can't claim to know how they feel even though I lost my dad when I was ten. I had the luxury of distance and trauma–my dad lived a thousand miles away, and a single, accidental gunshot took his life. For me, he just wasn't there anymore. For Tyler and Krysta, they had to say their goodbyes and I'm sure that's infinitely worse. When my dad died, no one came forward to tell me what a great guy he was, that was left largely to my limited memories and imagination. For Tyler and Krysta Bernasconi, though, I have the ability–I have the obligation–to tell them about their dad.

When he was twelve.

When he was fifteen.

When he was eighteen.

Something tells me he was a top-notch police officer, a loving husband, a wonderful dad. Something in my soul knows these things as fact. He was on the Board of the Visalia *Wish Upon A Star* organization, a foundation sponsored by California Law Enforcement personnel dedicated to granting wishes to children with catastrophic illnesses. This makes me smile.

It will take time for me to get over Ryan's death, though I will always be sad knowing that he was the first of the Monache High School class of 1986 to leave us.

God speed Ryan Bernasconi.

May 10, 2006

www.ingramcontent.com/pod-product-compliance
Lightning Source LLC
Chambersburg PA
CBHW031441040426
42444CB00007B/919